Bewitched & Beyond

THE FAN WHO CAME TO DINNER

BY MARK WOOD
WITH EDDIE LUCAS

BEWITCHED AND BEYOND:
THE FAN WHO CAME TO DINNER
©2013 MARK WOOD

ALL RIGHTS RESERVED.

No part of this book may be reproduced in any form or by any means, electronic, mechanical, digital, photocopying, or recording, except for inclusion of a review, without permission in writing from the publisher.

Published in the USA by:

BEARMANOR MEDIA
P.O. BOX 71426
ALBANY, GEORGIA 31708
www.BearManorMedia.com

ISBN-10: 1-59393-262-6 (alk. paper)
ISBN-13: 978-1-59393-262-6 (alk. paper)

DESIGN AND LAYOUT: VALERIE THOMPSON

Table of Contents

FOREWORD BY ROSE MARIE . . . 1

FOREWORD BY BERNARD FOX . . . 3

INTRODUCTION . . . 5

PROLOGUE . . . 7

CHAPTER 1: HOW I BECAME "BEWITCHED". . . 9

CHAPTER 2: THE YEAR THAT CHANGED MY LIFE . . . 15

CHAPTER 3: JOSIE IMOGENE ROGERS . . . 17

CHAPTER 4: THE PARAMOUNT YEARS . . . 23

CHAPTER 5: FROM PEYTON PLACE TO WESTPORT . . . 39

CHAPTER 6: SO, ON TO WESTPORT... . . . 43

CHAPTER 7: MOTOCROSS MAMA . . . 53

CHAPTER 8: MY BIG MOVE . . . 57

CHAPTER 9: WINK . . . 59

CHAPTER 10: CLIFTON AND INA . . . 63

CHAPTER 11: A PRECURSOR OF THINGS TO COME . . . 67

CHAPTER 12: SON OF A WITCH . . . 71

CHAPTER 13: WITCHES IN CLOUDS, MONSTERS IN TREES . . . 77

CHAPTER 14: THE POOP DECK . . . 79

CHAPTER 15: EARTHQUAKE '94 . . . 81

Chapter 16: **I Went to the Circus with Gladys Kravitz** ... 85

Chapter 17: **Samantha, Jeannie, and Jerry Springer** ... 99

Chapter 18: **Calling Dr. Bombay! Emergency! Come Right Away!** ... 103

Chapter 19: **An Adventure in Ventura** ... 111

Chapter 20: **Recipe for a Cookbook** ... 113

Chapter 21: **Agnes of God** ... 119

Chapter 22: **The Ides of March** ... 125

Chapter 23: **Alice Doesn't Live Here Anymore** ... 127

Chapter 24: **Kasey's Commercial** ... 131

Chapter 25: **America Gets a Step-Dad: The Second Darrin** ... 133

Chapter 26: **Farewell to the 1990s** ... 141

Chapter 27: **Bad Blood on the Set** ... 149

Chapter 28: **A Bit More *Bewitched...Again*** ... 153

Chapter 29: **The Glorious Gals of M-G-M** ... 157

Chapter 30: **A Decade with Kasey** ... 165

Chapter 31: **Spooky Happenings** ... 167

Chapter 32: **Wrapping Up The Years** ... 173

Chapter 33: **Poignant Goodbyes** ... 185

Epilogue ... 187

Acknowledgments ... 199

Index ... 201

FOREWORD
BY ROSE MARIE

I first met Kasey sometime in the mid 50's. I had hired her then husband, Bud Lewis, as my publicist.

I must admit, I don't recall much about that.

Flash forward 40 years when, out-of-the-blue, I got a call from Kasey.

It seems she and her new friend, Mark, had had some success with a cookbook about Bewitched and wondered if I would like to do one based on my character of Sally Rogers from the "Dick Van Dyke Show." It sounded fun so we met at a local coffee shop in the famed Sportsman's Lodge hotel.

I must admit, I don't recall much about that either.

Now, let me set you straight, the ol' memory is working just fine... it's just that not much came of both of those moments. Ha!

Oh well, such is the Creative World we live in.

Luckily we didn't let another 40 years go by and I was later involved in their projects "Son of A Witch" and its more copyrighted version, "Bewitched... Again" (in that one as Sally, believe it or not. Mark decided that it would be fun if McMann and Tate hired comedy writer Sally Rogers as their new copy writer)!

Again... not much came of that but we can blame the "powers that be" in Hollywood for not knowing a great idea when slapped across the face with it!!

When Kasey got sick Mark needed to earn some extra money as he had quit all his jobs to help her and I needed some help around the house.

Boy, did I create a monster... can't get rid of him! Lord knows I have tried. But, then again, I began to realize I felt my best when I was with him. God love him, he has gotten me to some of the best

doctors, takes me grocery shopping and fusses at me every time I eat something unhealthy... which, OK, OK, is most of the time, but don't tell him! He'll just fuss louder... what a whiner.

I love him!

And for that matter so does my daughter, "Noopy."

Go ahead, read his book. You won't find a better one about all of us and his time with Kasey. And for the record, Mark, honey, we all are bewitched...

...again.

Foreword
by Bernard Fox

Kasey and I never worked together on "Bewitched." Now, that is not to say we didn't share an episode together. We just never met. I believe she had magically turned into Samantha and I had to figure out how to turn her back. I have to agree with many of the fans that it would have been a better episode if the two actresses had actually changed parts for the spell to look more effective! Perhaps I had better luck with Macedonian Do-Do birds!

I digress.

It wasn't until her friend, Mark, arrived on the scene that we actually met. But the oddest thing about that reunion is the realization between Kasey and my lovely wife, Jacque, that they had known each other for years and years. I believe Mark tells about that somewhere amongst these pages so I won't ruin the tale here!

Through the years we all grew very close, dinners here, dinners out (that Mark sure can eat!) Kasey, poor love, used to go with us during one of her several bouts with cancer and drink only a nutritional drink... but she never complained and we always had a lovely time.

In May of 2006 my youngest daughter, Valerie, passed away quite unexpectedly. Kasey was very ill at the time and we didn't know that she would be gone from us as well just a month later. But what a trooper, she brought us a lovely garden statute of St. Francis and was even able to attend the funeral.

But enough of sadness... there are many stories in this book of happy times with *Mrs. Kravitz* and *Dr. Bombay* and Hallowe'en parties and even a St. Patrick's day gala when Kasey cooked a wonderful corned beef and cabbage... who would think that corned beef and cabbage could be wonderful?

Such lovely times.

And remember, my friends, if you ever don't feel quite up to par… I'm only a small spell away… and I'm sure all of you remember how it goes… "Calling Dr. Bombay! Calling Dr. Bombay…"

Introduction

Through the years, I've been told by a lot of people that my story is pretty unusual, and I guess I'd have to agree.

True, not just anyone can say that they met someone who starred in their favorite TV sitcom, fell in love with them, moved in together, and became an integral part of their life for the next fifteen years.

As fate would have it, I happen to be one of those minuscule few, and every day I thank my lucky stars!

People have been urging me for years to share these magical moments from our rather unconventional love story. So here they are—complete with all the fun, adventure, laughter, sadness, and heartache.

I hope you enjoy our special memories in *Bewitched and Beyond: The Fan Who Came to Dinner.*

Baby Imogene circa 1927

PROLOGUE
JULY 6TH, 2006

It was hot and sunny. Then again, when is it not in L.A.?

I was extremely exhausted and overwhelmed by every negative emotion known to man: fear, anger, stress, and unbelievable sadness.

SueAne Langdon was driving me through the streets of Hidden Hills desperately trying to distract me, by pointing out homes of the famous.

I had been too tired to even attempt to drive to the hospital that morning, so Sue offered to take me that afternoon. Not long after we were on our way, I received *the* dreaded phone call.

Kasey was gone.

This wonderful woman, known to the world as Louise Tate, the boss' wife on *Bewitched*, had lain in intensive care for six long days.

I had talked to her, sung to her ("Beautiful Dreamer"), held her hand, and told her that whatever needed to happen was okay.

Twice she had "reacted" to me by fighting to awaken. No one else had been lucky enough to experience that.

SueAne turned around and drove us back to her house. I collapsed on her day bed—the same day bed that Kasey and I had helped choose a new fabric for only a year or so earlier. The same day bed that Kasey sat on only six months prior, during her 80th birthday party, and taken the most wonderful photo alongside *Bewitched* alumni Bernard Fox and William Asher doing the "hear no evil, see no evil, say no evil" pose.

Lying there in a state of numbness, I found it hard to believe that Kasey was really gone.

Thank God for SueAne. She was there to help me through one of the saddest days of my life.

SueAne, words can never express my gratitude for all your help that day, and all the help you give still. You truly are a "best friend." Thank you.

Chapter 1
How I Became "Bewitched"

L-R William Asher, Elizabeth Montgomery, Dick York ponder the dialogue in a *Bewitched* script while standing in the garage set.

I was once asked, "Who do you think is actually "bewitched" in *Bewitched*?"

If you think about it, it's not Darrin. He isn't the recipient of some magic spell used to *make* him fall in love with the wrong woman, as was the case in the *Bewitched* precursor, *Bell, Book and Candle*. And sensible Samantha isn't the errant victim of her own love potion like Veronica Lake's "Jennifer," in *I Married a Witch*.

So who was really "bewitched"?

The answer is simple.

We were! We All were!

Samantha simply fell in love. I know exactly how she felt. Like Dorothy, who left the sepia-toned world of Kansas and ended up in the Technicolor world of Oz, I left Smyrna, Georgia and ended up in Tinsel Town. (Okay, close enough...) But being a tad smarter than Dorothy, I *never* wanted to go home. My favorite TV show of all-time was *Bewitched* and my favorite movie was *The Wizard of Oz*.

So early on I realized I have a thing about witches. I like the kind of witches that ride on brooms, appear on Hallowe'en candy ads, and sometimes have green faces... Samantha Stephens always had a great line that she'd use when telling someone her secret; "I am a witch. A real-live house haunting, broom riding, card-carrying, cauldron stirring, witch!" *Those* are the kind of witches I mean and I'll probably need a twelve step program to get over it!

One of the things I liked best about *Bewitched* was the fantasy and fun of being able to do anything *magical*. I wanted the powers and abilities they had! I can even twitch my nose... (I'd like to say it took years of practice, but who am I kidding? I could always do it! I'm also quite proud of the fact I am able to laugh every bit as loud and long as Margaret Hamilton!) Being a part of a generation whose chief babysitter was the television, I began to fall in love with the characters on that show.

Little did I know that many years later, I would end up meeting many of those same familiar faces I had grown up watching in my living room—Samantha, Tabatha, Darrin #2, Mrs. Kravitz, Esmeralda, Dr. Bombay, and the person who would eventually become my best friend and soul-mate, Kasey Rogers, better known to *Bewitched* fans as "the second Louise Tate."

It happened like that old saying: "through a friend of a friend"...

...In September of 1991, I met a young man named David Story who is the author of a wonderful book called *America on the Re-run*.

I shared with him my love of *Bewitched* and that I had an idea for a spin-off series called *Bewitched... Again!*. He, in turn, got me in touch with another author who had recently completed a book on *Bewitched*, and had some very important contacts, Herbie J Pilato (a name well known to *Bewitched* fans).

I called Herbie at his parent's home in New York State, and we had an enjoyable time sharing our mutual love and admiration for

all things *Bewitched*. During the course of our conversation, I also shared with him a synopsis of *Bewitched... Again!*. It went like this:

Adam Stephens; the product of a mixed marriage and son of Samantha and Darrin, wants to attend a MORTAL college like his father, much to the chagrin of his Aunt Enchantra, who prefers he go to MIC (Magic, Incantations and Conjuring).

Adam's best friend is Danny Kravitz, the nephew of neighbors Abner and Gladys. Adam is also engaged to a beautiful girl named Judy Hawthorne, who, as fate would have it, is a direct descendant of *THE* Hawthorne's, who had officiated over the Salem Witch Trials!

As you may notice, my story is a flip-flop of the original. This time around, it's the pretty *girl* that is mortal, and the boy who is the *witch*... er... *warlock*.

Through the ensuing years, the story line would change and adapt as Adam grew older and more of the original cast members passed away, but this was the original premise.

Herbie *loved* the idea and gladly gave me the home phone numbers of all the stars of *Bewitched!* Armed with the knowledge that Elizabeth Montgomery would have *nothing* to do with it, I still wanted to talk with someone who had been on the show. I wanted to get their honest reaction and see if anyone else would be even remotely interested in my spin-off.

I mulled over the list of phone numbers and decided to call Kasey Rogers; the only star on the list who didn't seem to intimidate me!

I finally worked up the nerve to call her and picked up the phone. I rehearsed my "pitch" as it was ringing. After a few rings, it went to the answering machine. And there it was... *her voice*; not lilting, but deeper and throatier, and still recognizable to *any Bewitched* fan.

After her message, I explained who I was and asked if she would be interested in reprising her role as Louise Tate on a project I was currently working on.

There! I had taken the first step, and had even gotten it all out before the "beep" went off! Now, I wondered if I'd hear anything back.

The next day, I came home from who-knows-where, and my mom said, "Mark, your friend Kasey called."

"Kasey?" I said, thinking out loud. "I don't know any "Kasey"...

Two seconds later it hit me and I responded with an "OH MY GAWD!"! Immediately I ran to the phone to return her call.

Nervously, I dialed her number and this time she answered!

To say we hit it off from the get-go would be an understatement. Almost an hour later, we were still chatting away on the phone. Thus was the beginning of my journey on the road to finding that proverbial soul mate! Then again, it was Kasey's road as well. We just didn't know it yet!

Kasey Rogers... Louise Tate... The boss' wife from *Bewitched*— This is the woman who would eventually become my *everything*... And over the course of the next fifteen years she did exactly that.

Now, before I go any further, I will clear up that burning question that people are always wondering but [sometimes] too polite to ask; "Was your relationship sexual?"

The answer is, "NO." Kasey and I were not sexually involved. I am not now, nor have I ever been what is referred to as a "boy-toy"! I'm the first to admit that I don't have the body for it... then again, in my circle, anyone who drives after dark is considered a stud! HA!

For some reason, most people can't seem to fathom a perfect "marriage" without sex. But believe it or not, Kasey and I had it.

I remember her initially hoping that I would be someone her youngest daughter could "get to know"... But all that was immediately cleared up at the now defunct Queen of Cups Tea-room in Venice Beach, where we once had our tea leaves read by a psychic.

The last word on the subject is this: You can count the *straight* fans of *Bewitched* on one hand.

Enough said.

Laura Elliot (Kasey) with M-G-M's first big star: the original Leo the Lion. I probably should have put this photo first as all good pictures started with his roar! LOL

Chapter 2
THE YEAR THAT CHANGED MY LIFE

It was September, 1991, when I made that initial phone call to Kasey. By the following Hallowe'en, I found myself in Los Angeles for a small meeting set up at Columbia Pictures, which at that time was not yet owned by Sony, but still on its original lot at Sunset/Gower in Hollywood.

Kasey and I spoke constantly by phone until then. Herbie Pilato also flew out, so it was our first face-to-face meeting as well. We all made plans to meet at a restaurant in Burbank named Chadney's (since closed for years).

Herbie and I walked in together, and there she was. I can still remember what she was wearing—a long, fuzzy, pink and white sweater, and pink leggings… she looked great, and that picture will stay in my mind forever. Hugs all around and then we enjoyed a pleasant lunch as we began preparing our plan of attack on Columbia!

During my visit, I would be staying with my sister, who lived near Disneyland some sixty miles away, but still close enough that I could drive up to Kasey's every day. Since I was to be there over Hallowe'en, I brought along some costumes all the way from Smyrna. (And back then, I couldn't imagine why Kasey wasn't interested in going out on Hallowe'en with some guy she had just met who brought costumes from home!)

As you might guess, that was one Hallowe'en I spent sitting at home. Even my own sister wouldn't go anywhere with me!

The next day we arrived together at the Studio. I think the guy who had once told me: "anytime you come out look me up, we'll chat" was taken aback that I had actually done it as our initial meeting at Columbia was met with a bit of resistance. But Kasey and I still kept a positive attitude and "just knew" that we had them in our back pocket (Ahh, the faith of the young and young at heart). We were given a small tour of the studio, saw the sound stages where *Bewitched* and *I Dream of Jeannie* (among so much more) were filmed and got to actually see inside Harry Cohen's office.

A QUICK SIDE NOTE about the original Czar of Columbia Pictures; In his day, Harry Cohen was NOT well liked. He would bark orders from his office window at all the writers. If he did not hear the sounds of typing, you were out! His wife was his secretary and sat out front of his office. This did not detour Harry and his womanizing ways, the man who made stars of Rita Hayworth (and later Kim Novak when he got angry at Hayworth) simply had a secret staircase put into a small closet in his personal office. If Mrs. Cohen ever knew about the hopeful starlets he paraded in and out of there she never said a word!

ON ANOTHER FUN NOTE, whether it was a recreation or not, the office used for Darrin's psychiatrist in an episode from season 3 called "No More Mr. Nice Guy" was the exact same in look as Mr. Cohen's. Even the doorknobs, Aunt Clara, are the same as on set!

After that initial let-down, I went back to Smyrna, Herbie went back to New York, but Kasey and I continued to chat every day.

Chapter 3
JOSIE IMOGENE ROGERS

I'd like to tell you a bit about the "early" Kasey. "Kasey" was a stage name; her third, as a matter of fact.

She was born Josie Imogene (pronounced "EYE-mo-gene" in this case) Rogers in Moorehouse, Missouri on December 15, 1925; not

Imogene graduated from Burbank High soon after playing the lead in her high school play, *The Taming of the Shrew*. Her leading "man" was her best girlfriend, because most of the available boys had gone to war.

1926, as some bios have reported. The confusion in age began when she went to Paramount and decided to shave a year off, as the life span of the starlet is so short.

Her parents were Eben Elijah and Ina Mae Rogers—he being from Illinois, and she from Kentucky.

At the age of two, the Rogers family left Missouri and moved to Los Angeles to a home on 61st Street. By the time Kasey was twelve, they were living in Burbank. (Kasey once figured that she had lived in at least *thirty-six* different homes in her lifetime!)

It was here in grade school, that she discovered she could hit a baseball farther than any boy, and they tagged her with the nickname "Casey." It would be many years later when her second husband would change the "C" to a "K."

Shortly after, she became engaged to a young man from Scotland named Tommy, whose family had recently moved to California. Because he was Scottish, Tommy couldn't fight for America, so he enlisted in the RAF (Royal Air Force) instead.

Kasey kept all his letters and a few mementos until just a few months before her death. I never read them, but she once told me that he sounded increasingly frightened about a huge secret mission he was about to go on.

Imogene and Tommy.

Tommy's uneasy feelings may have been a premonition because the plane he commandeered on that very mission went down under mysterious circumstances and Imogene never saw him again. Tommy was only twenty years old.

We spent many hours in the last year of Kasey's life trying to find out what had happened to Tommy, but never did. Kasey harbored some guilt over thoughts she had of breaking off the engagement, but Tommy, at least in this lifetime, never knew of her intentions.

Imogene later married James Donnellan after briefly dating his brother. Albeit too late, she ultimately realized, and freely admitted, that she had married the wrong Donnellan!

About this same time, a talent scout from Paramount Pictures had seen Kasey working as a show girl (under the name "Sandy Donnellan") at the Earl Carroll Theatre.

Kasey aka Sandy Donnellan is on the right.

An Earl Carroll Girl was Hollywood's answer to Broadway's Ziegfeld Girl. Earl Carroll Girls were gorgeous, leggy, and performed entertaining song and dance revues on an 80-foot main stage with a 60-foot wide double revolving circular stage that rotated in two different directions. As a matter of fact, the theater is still there on Sunset Boulevard.

> FUN SIDE NOTE: In the mid-1990s, Kasey, Sandra Gould, (the second "Gladys Kravitz") and Bernard Fox ("Dr. Bombay"), once did a talk show on that very stage. During one of the breaks, Kasey began looking around backstage, and found what was left of this amazing revolving stage from decades before. She excitedly showed it to us and the crew members who were working there. Because the theater had been turned into a sound stage a few years before, no one working there at the time had ever noticed what was left of this amazing DOUBLE revolving stage from a Hollywood long gone by.

It was during this time that Imogene also found out she was pregnant. To her, that situation was a no-brainer. She quickly decided that taking care of her baby was much more important than the talent scout, or being a movie star at Paramount, so she passed. Can you imagine?!

Many determined actresses would have not even considered passing as an option.

On December sixteenth, one day after her twenty-first birthday, Imogene gave birth to a little baby boy named after his father, James, but who would always be called "Jay."

Chapter 4
THE PARAMOUNT YEARS

Laura Elliot

Less than a year later, with her marriage in shreds, Kasey decided to throw caution to the wind and call the Paramount talent scout to ask if he'd still be interested.

Top left is soon-to-be TV's Superman, George Reeves. William Eyeth is in the center with KR on his left.

Amazingly, he said yes (one lucky girl, here!) and a screen test was set up opposite none other than Paramount legend, Charles Boyer! (Today, that would be like going on YOUR FIRST EVER audition and reading with Brad Pitt!)

And if that wasn't amazing enough, only three days later, she found herself co-starring opposite future "Superman," George Reeves, in her first film called *Special Agent*. The film also starred William Eyeth, who was writing a little show at the time called *Lend an Ear*.

Lend An Ear would be the stage play that would ultimately propel Carol Channing to stardom.

FUN NOTE: Fifty years later, Kasey and I went to see Carol recreate her legendary role of Dolly Levi at the Pasadena Playhouse. She was amazing! When she descended the staircase singing "Hello Dolly," the audience rose to their feet and roared with approval—and didn't stop! For what seemed to be an amazingly long time, Carol just *stood* there! Then, slowly she picked up her skirt and train, and went *back up the stairs*, pointed to the band, and did it all over again! This time, the audience went even wilder!

Finally, in loving desperation, she went to the edge of the stage, motioned for everyone to quiet down and simply stated, "I'd like to go on, but you won't shut-up!"

After the show, we went backstage and Kasey told Carol of her experience with Bill Eyeth and *Lend An Ear*. Carol, who was very sweet, smiled, and then very tongue in cheek, told Kasey that it was *impossible* because Kasey couldn't be old enough to remember all that! Carol is something else!

Pressured by Paramount to change her name, Josie Imogene Rogers Donnellan became "Laura Elliot." She chose "Laura," because she liked the song from the movie of the same name, and thought the film's star, Gene Tierney, absolutely gorgeous. The surname "Elliott" was suggested by a studio executive.

Armed with a new name and one of Hollywood's leading studios, Laura Elliott would go on to make twenty-eight films and become a part of Paramount's second Golden Circle.

Laura was the only starlet to be put under contract that year but soon others followed, and to the New Golden Circle came the likes of Barbara Rush, Ann Robinson, and Peter Hansen.

Kasey remembered, "We all did studio promotions together. You can also find us altogether in several Paramount films including *A Place in the Sun*, and the original *War of the Worlds*. We got to work with some of the biggest names in the business; George Stevens, Frank Capra, C.B. DeMille! It was great fun."

Although Laura and the others didn't have very much to do in these films, they were grateful for the opportunity to be there, and found them great learning experiences.

Many years later, at a long forgotten function, Kasey was asked to stand up and talk about working with film legends Elizabeth Taylor and Montgomery Clift from *A Place in the Sun*. Not having a clue what to say (because she didn't even remember having met them on the *one* day she was on set) she quipped, "Well, let's see...

Paramount's 2nd Golden Circle.

Take the "Elizabeth" from Taylor and the "Montgomery" from Clift and you have *Elizabeth Montgomery*. Let's talk about *Bewitched*!" She got a big laugh but then honestly admitted she was only on set one day during a party scene and didn't remember too much about it.

But Laura's biggest film was yet to come: Warner Bros. adaptation of the Patricia Highsmith novel, *Strangers on a Train* directed by the legendary Alfred Hitchcock.

"Is your name, Miriam?"

"Why, yes!"

In 2003, fifty years later, "Laura" was re-united for the first time with co-star Farley Granger at a screening of "Strangers" at the Egyptian Theatre in Los Angeles. Farley, who was eighty-something at the time, was still quite handsome and dapper and charming as ever.

Laura played Miriam; Farley Granger's bitchy, conniving wife, who quickly gets her come-uppance at the hands of an insane Robert Walker, in his last major role.

The demise of Miriam is reflected in the glasses that fall from her face as Bruno strangles her. Kasey actually kept a pair of those glasses and today they reside in a small museum of Hollywood memorabilia called Movie Madness Museum in Oregon. They were given to the owner, Michael Clark, by Kasey, who was a friend.

In 2004 when Michael was in Los Angeles, we all went on a "field trip" and found the location that had been used as the carnival site in *Strangers*. Today, it is covered by a large housing development, but the lake on which they rode into the tunnel of love is still there!

Kasey recalled one of her cousins going to see the film with friends, and how embarrassed she was by Kasey's *bad girl* antics. "My cousin denied even knowing me in the film and slunk down in her seat!" Kasey laughed. "Well, I *was* pretty risqué in that film." (Just watch her eat the ice cream cone...) Even Kasey admitted to not realizing what "Hitch" was going for until many years later. "I was so square then!" she'd say.

Kasey relished her role in *Strangers*, and always loved playing the bad girl. "It was always so much more fun!"

One favorite memory Kasey had was during the strangulation scene. It was filmed on a large, bare soundstage with a camera pointing into a big, concave mirror. Nothing on the set; no tree, no Robert Walker, as seen in the finished production.

Hitchcock sat in his director chair and simply said, "Laura, float backwards to the ground." "Yes, Mr. Hitchcock," she replied. So she "floated" backwards a bit and then THUD!—landed on the hard, cement floor.

"Laura, *float* to the floor," was his one and only response and line of direction. So she got up and did it again... and again... and again. Finally, on the *seventh* take, she somehow managed to float *all* the way to the floor. Hitchcock simply said "Cut," and that was it.

The amazing thing about the shot is the lack of Robert Walker and the tree reflected in the sunglasses. Those elements were added in post-production. Many times I attended film school lectures with Kasey and she would explain to the students how the scene was shot, compared to what they saw in the actual film.

One thing Kasey was VERY proud of, but didn't know until many years later, was that Hitchcock was once quoted in the book, *Hitchcock*, by Truffaut, as saying, "The gal who played the wife was particularly good." It's a shame he never said it directly to *her*. But he did tell her, "Lose ten pounds and you could play leads!" Laura took his constructive criticism seriously and found Hitchcock to be right, as many leading roles were soon to follow.

It was during this time that Laura also met and briefly dated Conrad Hilton, wealthy and affluent owner of the prosperous chain of Hilton Hotels. (Imagine if that particular situation had panned out: Kasey would've been Elizabeth Taylor AND Zsa Zsa Gabor's *mother-in-law*, as well as Paris Hilton's Grandmother…or Great Grandmother?! Well, something like that).

In August of 1999, Hollywood celebrated the 100th anniversary of Hitchcock's birthday, in which we attended several parties. Most Hitchcock fans never knew what happened to "Laura Elliot" since she had been re-christened "Kasey Rogers" many years earlier.

At one party, held on the roof top at the Academy of Motion Picture Arts and Sciences on August 13, 1999, we found Tippi Hedren "holding court" with several rapt fans and reporters. Suddenly one reporter saw Kasey and recognized her as *Laura*. Much to her amazement, every fan, every reporter, every photographer moved *en masse*, away from Miss Hedren and over to Kasey. The *buzz* of that evening became, "We never knew Louise Tate was Miriam!" So the long lost Laura Elliott had at last been found alive and well, but I'm not sure Tippi ever forgave us.

Another party was held in the forecourt of Grauman's Egyptian Theatre and in attendance was Patricia Hitchcock. She played Ruth Roman's kid sister in *Strangers* and Kasey had not seen her in nearly fifty years.

Pat Hitchcock is a very nice lady and a lot of fun. When I remarked how much I liked our table centerpiece, she insisted that I take it! I still have the bowl, and Kasey and I later used it in one of our Hallowe'en craft books.

Sadly, at yet another screening of *Strangers* during the 1999 celebration, we received word that Ruth Roman had passed away just moments earlier.

In July of 2005 we attended another Hitchcock function in San Francisco, and appeared on stage with Pat Hitchcock and Tippi Hedren. It was Kasey's last public appearance.

You've gotta hand it to Kasey. There she was living with a tracheostomy tube in her throat to breathe and a G-Tube in her stomach for eating, and she still looked *fantastic*!

Kasey enjoyed having people recognize her as Laura, which was at first rare, but now, it was becoming common knowledge that Laura and Kasey were the same gal.

As "Laura Elliot," she also made a handful of Westerns while at Paramount. Produced by Nat Holt, they included *Denver & the Rio*

"Laura" meets Tippi

"Laura" was also cast as she bore a resemblance to Patricia Hitchcock at the time.(A plot ploy in "Strangers on A Train" that nearly sets off Robert Walker to murder again)

"Laura" with another film fatale—Janet Leigh.

Grande, with Edmond O'Brien, Dean Jagger, J. Carroll Nash, and ZaSu Pitts, and *Silver City*, also with Edmond O'Brien, and Yvonne DeCarlo ("Lily Munster").

Kasey remembered Yvonne making sure that EVERYONE on set knew she had just been voted the "Most Beautiful Woman in the World," and apparently was a big pain in the ass about it.

Many years later, in 1996, Kasey and I went to an awards function in Antelope Valley and Yvonne DeCarlo was there as well. Kasey looked svelte and lovely in a beautiful sequined gown, and Yvonne… well… Yvonne looked like the golden cow they worshiped in the *Ten Commandments*. She didn't immediately recognize Kasey, but later when Kasey was on stage speaking, she mentioned that she had worked with Yvonne many years before in *Silver City*. I happened to be sitting within earshot and heard Yvonne say,

Kasey and Yvonne DeCarlo from *Silver City*

"*That's* where I know her from!" It suddenly dawned on her who Kasey was. Yvonne quickly made a few disparaging remarks (one inferring that Kasey had been quite "popular" with all the stunt men on the set), then suddenly "took ill," and left in quite a huff. (Smile.)

FUN NOTE: Producer Nat Holt had a daughter named Jacqueline, who Laura met on the set of one of the Westerns. Years later, "Jacque," grew up to marry Bernard Fox ("Dr. Bombay") from *Bewitched*! While Kasey only did one episode of *Bewitched* with Bernard, the two never actually met, as they never had any scenes together.

Sometime after I arrived in L.A., I finally got Bernard and Kasey together. During the meeting, both Jacque and Kasey looked at each other at the same time and said, "I know you!" and it suddenly became apparent from where. Small world, huh?

L to R- Edmund O'Brien, KR, J. Carrol Naish in *Denver and The Rio Grande*.

In the movie *Denver & the Rio Grande*, a massive train wreck was filmed. Two antique Victorian locomotives were smashed together, which actually brought tears to the eyes of several old, grizzled train engineers who were watching off-camera. However, before doing so, the trains were stripped of all their finery.

Actress ZaSu (pronounced ZAY-zoo) Pitts saved a bell from one of the trains, and Laura kept a beautiful hanging lamp from one of the dining cars. One of her sons still has it today. Later, one of the wrecked trains was refurbished and today resides at Knott's Berry Farm where you can still ride it and see Laura's picture, which hangs in their depot.

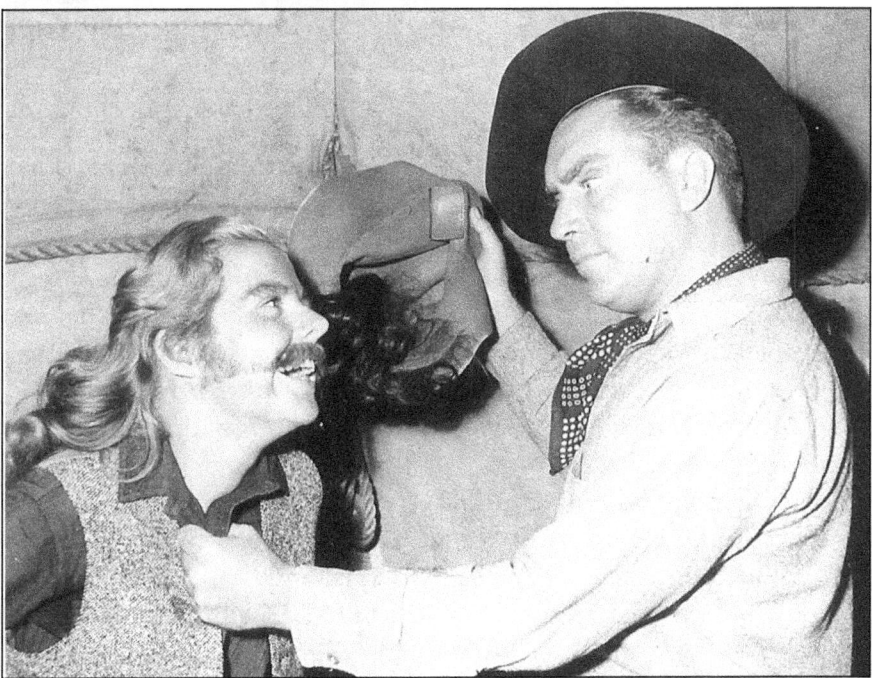

On July 28, 1951, as a prank, Kasey had the make-up team on "Denver and The Rio Grande" turn her into a grizzled ol' cow-poke. Then she had the stunt crew teach her how to "take a punch." They staged and filmed a fight scene, as this series of candid photos show, that did not make the final cut as her cowboy hat flew off revealing her blonde hair. Producer, Nat Holt was NOT amused that his female lead nearly got herself killed...or worse...BRUISED (as that would show)!

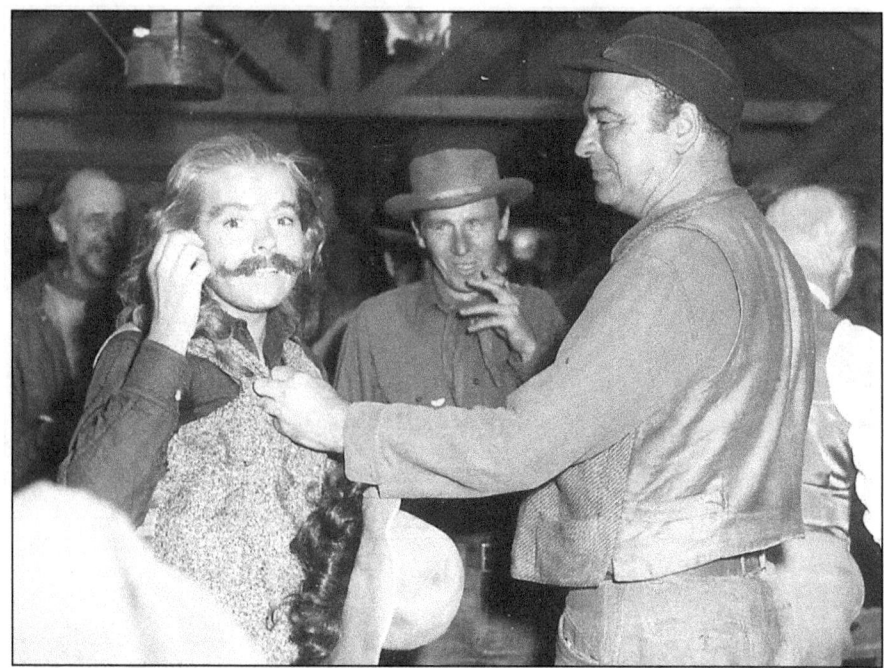

You really should check out these mid-century Westerns. They are beautifully photographed, the color pristine and the vistas are stunningly gorgeous.

Kasey/Laura went on to star and co-star in films such as *Sampson and Delilah* (she loved her one scene in that, when she asks the man with her why he doesn't gaze at her the same way he looks at Delilah he responds "You're NOT Delilah!" HA!), *Jamaica Run, Ask Any Girl* and her favorite "clunker," *Two Lost Worlds* with an unknown Jim Arness.

After her Paramount contract was up, Laura met and hired a publicist to help her career. His name was Walter "Bud" Lewis and he would later become her second husband, as well as the one responsible for changing her name from "Laura Elliott" to "Kasey Rogers."

In retrospect, Kasey felt it was a poor decision that ultimately divided her career in half.

Although it was the end of "Laura's" movie career, it was also the beginning of "Kasey's" successful career on television; one that would eventually boast over six-hundred leads and appearances on the small-screen throughout the fifties and sixties.

KASEY ROGERS

This is the last professional head shot that Kasey had made... it was always both of our favorites and I still have the raggedy jacket she wore in it.

Chapter 5
FROM PEYTON PLACE TO WESTPORT

Kasey's television career really hit the mother lode when she won the role of Julie Anderson in ABC's, *Peyton Place*. This controversial series was America's original primetime soap-opera and the forerunner to shows like *Dallas, Dynasty, Falcon Crest,* and *Knot's Landing.*

When the show premiered in 1964, it took the nation by storm because it was the first of its kind to talk about sex and infidelity in such an open and frank manner. By today's standards it seems incredibly tame, but not to a world where Lucy Ricardo and June Cleaver were the norm.

Peyton Place originally aired twice a week. It wasn't long before its ratings zoomed into the top twenty, eventually prompting ABC to order *three* episodes a week; quite unheard of at the time. Imagine a primetime series that aired three new episodes every week, with no reruns! Today, we're lucky if we get nine new episodes a season.

In the premiere episode, Kasey's character, Julie Anderson (Barbara Parkins' mother), is caught kissing Leslie Carrington (Paul Langton); a married man she works for and father to Ryan O'Neal's character.

To complicate matters, Julie is married to a man called "Crazy George" (played by Henry Beckman), which only adds to the drama. Once again, Kasey was playing the bad girl. However, this bad girl would soon be known all over the world because of the immense popularity of the series. "I remember getting off a plane in Lima, Peru and all I heard was 'Hola, Julie Anderson! Hola!'"

FUN SIDE NOTE: Many years later, dear friends of ours, Steve and Thomas, decided to throw a huge surprise party at Raleigh

Where's Rodney?

Studios in Hollywood, honoring Kasey's career. Steve and Thomas contacted as many people from Kasey's past as they could find. Unfortunately, most were either gone or had serious health issues and could not attend. This included *Gunsmoke* star, James Arness. Contrary to popular belief, Arness' first film was NOT *The Thing*. It was a really *bad* film called *Two Lost World's*, the vehicle for Kasey's third starring role and his first! Though the film was full of pirates, ship wrecks, volcanoes, and dinosaurs, even Kasey had to admit it was a stinker.

CHAPTER 5: FROM PEYTON PLACE TO WESTPORT | 41

Production still from *Two Lost Worlds*. Of interest is the built up platform that holds the volcano and backdrop on the soundstage. Kasey spent most of the time flipping her long hair around and ends up changing Arness' name half way thru the film! Where was the Continuity Girl on that day??

Henry Beckman (her husband on *Peyton Place* and who would later guest-star on *Bewitched*) attended the party with his son, traveling all the way from Washington State. Henry and Kasey had not seen each other since their Peyton Place days and the reunion was a lot of fun. Sadly, Henry's son passed away quite unexpectedly soon after and we never saw Henry again. Henry passed away 2 years after Kasey on June 17, 2008.

Kasey enjoyed working on *Peyton Place*, but remembers it was rather daunting at first, appearing for the first time as the mother of a teenager. Luckily, it wasn't long before her worries began to subside, and she began to relish her time on *Peyton Place*. "It was much more fun and relaxed than *Bewitched*," she later told me.

Kasey recalled there was once a rather complicated scene involving over thirty cast members and extras. "It was amazing. We had to 'block' the scene with all these different camera angles and characters. It was supposed to be one long continuous shot. We rehearsed it, broke for lunch, then came back and did it. And we did it in one take! We were all so surprised and proud, that we darn near ruined the end due to the excitement of it all!"

Also during her time on *Peyton Place*, Kasey was there to witness Mia Farrow's infamous hair-cutting incident. "Mia was so angered over not being able to join Frank Sinatra overseas for an Easter vacation because of her *Peyton Place* schedule, that after one of the rehearsals, she went in her dressing room and chopped off all of her gorgeous auburn hair! Practically down to the *roots*! I guess she was thinking, 'That'll mess up continuity enough to get me a few days off.' But Paul Monash [the director] took one look at her and said, 'Write it in!' and walked away. Poor Mia had to work anyway, but it gave her a stunning new look and a lot of publicity—things which both lasted a lot longer than her affair with Frank!"

Unfortunately by 1966, the bloom was off Kasey's character, and Betty's mother was written off the show. Sadly, she was also never included in any of the subsequent *Peyton Place* films, which hurt her deeply.

Chapter 6
So, On to Westport...

Larry gives his new wife the "once-over"!

For the first two seasons of *Bewitched*, an actress named Irene Vernon played the part of Louise Tate, but as she would soon find out, there were many changes brewing on the set of *Bewitched*.

Director (later producer) William Asher and wife, *Bewitched* star Elizabeth Montgomery, had now taken over the reins of the show and were doing a bit of house cleaning.

Not only was the show to debut in color for its third season, the new producers also felt that Larry Tate needed a younger, "trophy wife." So, it was goodnight Irene, Kasey's up to bat!

Kasey doffs the black wig after filming scenes in episode #106, *Nobody But A Frog Knows How to Live*.

"*Bewitched* was one of my favorite shows before I got to be on it," Kasey told me. "It was a real thrill. I didn't even have to read for the part. I just went in, met with Harry [Ackerman] and Bill [Asher], and the next week I was 'Louise!' At first, it was kind of a challenge to go from all the 'internalizing' of *Peyton Place*, to the wide eyed comedic innocence of Louise Tate yelling, 'Larry!'

I also donned a dark wig so the change in actresses wouldn't be quite as noticeable. I wore that dark wig until Dick Sargent took over the role of Darrin. It used to itch and bother me. You can even see me scratching at it from time to time in some of the episodes.

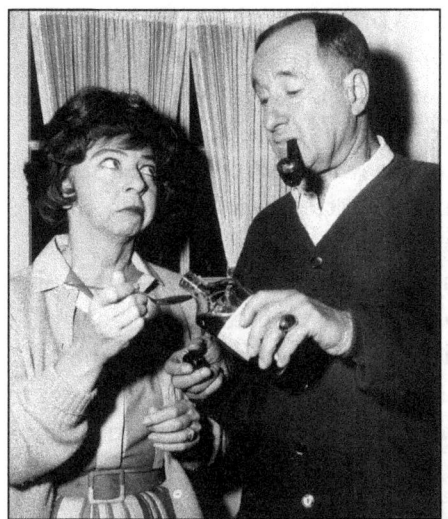 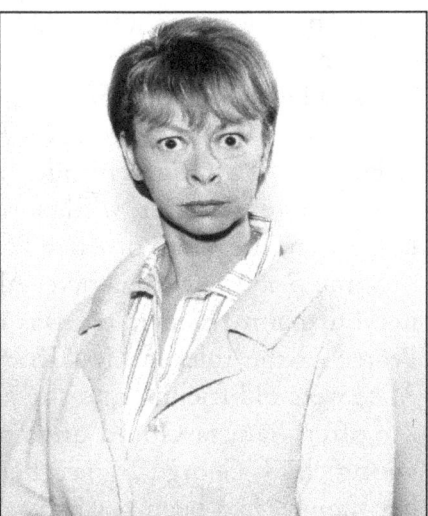

The Kravitz's: Alice Pearce + Mary Grace Canfield = Sandra Gould!

So one day, in make-up, I asked Bill if I had to keep wearing it and he remarked he didn't even know why I was wearing it to begin with! So that's how Louise became a red-head overnight!"

Other changes on the show included a new "Gladys Kravitz." Sandra Gould would replace Alice Pearce, who had passed away from cancer at the end of the previous season.

The producers, as well as the network, didn't like the idea of an older married couple getting divorced, and in a situation comedy, the sudden death of one of the main characters was out of the question, so the role of Gladys Kravitz had to be recast.

For a few transition episodes, actress Mary Grace Canfield played Abner's sister, Harriet, while a suitable actress was found to fill the larger than life shoes of Alice Pearce.

Some *Bewitched* trivia here: Alice Ghostley, who would later play nervous nanny Esmeralda, was offered the chance to replace Alice Pearce in the role of Mrs. Kravitz, but declined because she and Alice were old friends, and she just didn't feel right about accepting the offer. Sandra Gould once told me that when she had been a young child, George Tobias (her on screen hubby and fifteen years her senior), had been her baby sitter!

Along with the new color episodes, came a new look. Samantha no longer wore the full-skirted, shirt-waist dresses of the "Donna Reed" era, but sported a sleeker, sixties look; not too "mod" but pleasantly "hip."

Also gone was the bow Elizabeth wore on the back of her head which pulled up the sides of her hair. (I always missed that... Next time you watch an episode, notice that her hair is even *drawn* that way in the opening cartoon credits, although the bow is undoubtedly hidden under her pointed hat!)

"I was very glad to be on *Bewitched*, but it wasn't always a happy set," Kasey would say. "I wasn't privy to a lot of what was going on, but when the Asher 'take-over' came, there was a lot of bad feelings that took time to dissipate.

I remember one time I was to wear a fur coat in a scene. I didn't really have a dressing room because I wore all my own clothes on the show and make-up was in a different building, so I asked a crew member for a place to hang the coat between shots. But I might as well have been talking to a brick wall. I didn't get anywhere and guess I was looking a little frustrated when Elizabeth came over and asked if I needed anything. I told her, 'Yes,' I needed somewhere to hang up this expensive coat. A moment later the same crew member came over, hammered a big nail in the side of a flat and walked off. I had to hang this *beautiful* fur coat on a nail on a flat! Incredibly friendly place, huh?!!"

Kasey and Sandy Gould at a mixed drink competition in the late 1960s.

Kasey also told me many times that she "had to sit through take after take of that *dreadful* "Iffin" song," (Hippie, Hippie, Hooray).

And she recalled a Halloween episode where Elizabeth comes into the room and accidentally spills a drink down her entire front, which was not supposed to happen. "She never stopped. It was only water (supposedly the pre-requisite martini), and it must've been cold, but she just kind of wiped it away and kept going. You can still see that on the episode. I have to say that Liz was a consummate pro."

Elizabeth Montgomery could sometimes be a tad mischievous. Kasey recalled a particular scene at the Stephens' dinner table. "It was the last shot of the day, and even though I know everybody thinks we drank like fish on the show, we didn't. The characters did, but the actors didn't. Let me clear the air right here, 'booze' is always faked. *Except* in this one shot, Liz had replaced the fake wine with *Sangria* and nobody knew! We sat down at the table and the cameras began to roll. We were saying our lines and one by one, we all took a drink, realized, and all looked over at Liz who had this impish little grin on her face the entire time.

I also remember Bill wrapping up the filming of another evening's shoot because I was running late to catch a cruise ship. I know a lot of people, such as Sandra Gould, had problems with Bill, but I always adored him and was never treated any way by him except nice...

...but then again, there was this one time... I could've shot him! It's a scene in the Tate's bedroom. This was actually just Samantha and Darrin's own bedroom, redressed. Anyway, I'm at the dressing table getting ready to go out [from the episode "Art For Sam's Sake"], and Larry is in the bathroom coming out from the shower rubbing his hair with a towel.

Well, David [White] had had a bit too much to drink the night before, and this was the first shot of the day. He was still 'flying' and got rather *promiscuous* with me. He kept picking me up and throwing me down on the bed over and over. It was awful! And no one, not even Bill, came to my rescue! David just thought it was all so funny. But it wasn't funny to me. Finally things calmed down, we got the shot and I got out of there!

But things did eventually settle down and the show became more fun," she added.

Kasey was the center of attention in one particular episode that many fans remember called "Mona Sammy." In this episode, Larry and Louise are over for dinner and notice a 'Mona Lisa' style portrait of Samantha hanging over the fireplace. This had been a gift from Endora, and was originally signed by Leonardo da Vinci. Noticing Louise being quite taken with it, the ever-mischievous Endora casts a spell and changes the signature on the portrait to "Darrin Stephens." This causes Louise to insist that Darrin paint her. Not

Kasey poses in June of 2003 with the two portraits of her used in *Bewitched*. Die-hard fans may also recognize the dress she is wearing. Kasey wore this as Louise in Season 3's first episode: *I Remember You Sometimes*. 34 years later she could proudly still get into it!

taking no for an answer, Samantha and Darrin finally agree by deciding that Samantha will put a spell on Darrin, so he can paint a lovely portrait of Louise. Endora gets wind of what is going on, and changes Darrin's exquisite portrait of Louise into one that is quite HIDEOUS.

Kasey in *Bewitched*, 34 years earlier!

This episode would require two oil paintings of Louise Tate ("the pretty one and the goofy one" as Kasey and I always called them.) Many people ask if Kasey had to do a sitting for the artist. The answer is no. They took Polaroid shots of Kasey in different poses and then both portraits were painted from them by someone in the Screen Gems art department.

Kasey loved that episode and said, "I remember asking Bill if I could have the paintings after the shoot. He said 'Yes,' and I still have them."

I was lucky enough to be given these same portraits by Kasey, and I will treasure them always.

CHAPTER 6: SO, ON TO WESTPORT...

The "pretty one" always hung over the piano in the living room of the condo we shared. But every Halloween, we'd have a party and switch the "pretty one" for the "ugly one." God, what fun!

I once asked Kasey what she thought Louise Tate would be doing today. "Well, Larry's gone unfortunately, so Louise took over the company. She probably runs McMann and Tate, or has the lackey's do it. She's cruising Beverly Hills and Rodeo Drive in her Rolls you know, doing a little shopping... That's where Louise is today."

Well, almost! When I first got out to California Kasey was driving a navy blue Jag. What a kick! She hated driving so guess who got to drive us around in that?!

Kasey often related tales from her days in show biz and one of those stories included TV's undisputable Queen of Comedy, Lucille Ball.

Kasey had done *The Lucy Show* on a few occasions, remember the episode where she is to be the flight instructor for Lucy and Carol Burnett (when they decide to become stewardesses)? In another she played the wife of Phil Harris. Her part was *huge*. Kasey was thrilled! But Lucy wasn't.

At the table reading the first day, she recalled watching Lucy turn redder and redder, and I'm not talking her hair.

Finally, Lucy slammed the script down and stated emphatically, "We *don't* have a show" and left.

The next day when Kasey reported to the set, she could only laugh when she saw that her part had dwindled to a few simple lines. Her reaction? "Oh well, it isn't my show!" Forever the good sport!

Kasey also recalled a time when she and Lucy were walking out of the studio together on their way to get something to eat. Lucy suddenly stopped and asked Kasey if she thought herself to be a good mother. Kasey replied, "I sure hope so." Rather bluntly, Lucy stated "I'm an awful one"! The conversation didn't really go much past that but Kasey always felt Lucy thought she had failed greatly in that department.

SOME FUN TRIVIA: *Peyton Place* and *Bewitched* both premiered on ABC back in 1964. At the time, *Peyton Place* was considered very "racey," but let's answer the age-old question, "Who was the first TV couple to share the same bed?" It's usually considered a toss-up between Herman and Lily Munster and Darrin and Samantha Stephens. Many have tried to lay claim to that "position," but truth be told, the first to actually spend the night next to each other in televised holy matrimony was none other than Fred and Wilma Flintstone!

Chapter 7
MOTOCROSS MAMA

Kasey in 1971 astride her first motorcycle: a Honda 500 IV Original.

Some of you may not know that Kasey Rogers was one of the founding pioneers of Women's Motocross Racing!

Can't picture it?! Neither could I at first.... (Imagine Louise Tate wearing leather and slinging gravel...) But it became one of her greatest passions in life, and one of her proudest accomplishments.

How did Mrs. Larry Tate segue into leather? In the early seventies, her son, Mike, came home one day and announced that he wanted to get a motorcycle. Kasey's initial reaction was, "You want a *WHAT*?!" But he was determined to have one, and with a bit of convincing, Kasey relented and Mike got his motor-bike.

Since Mike's father seemed to have no interest in any of it, Kasey would take him up to Encino Hills where he could learn how to ride. Mike, was a fast learner and getting better with each passing day, so it wasn't long before he told his mom that he wanted to start racing.

"You want to *WHAT*?!"

Mike was a natural, and Kasey was impressed with his abilities so before long they traded Encino Hills for Indian Dunes, a 600 acre motorcycle park where he could practice dune racing on the weekends. It was there that he won the first race he ever competed in. Eventually, Mike would become a member of the upper echelon of cycle racing; one of the top five mini-cycle racers in the United States!

What did Kasey think of the sport? "I didn't like it at first," she told me. "It was muddy, and dirty, and LOUD. But after a while, I got tired of sitting there knitting and watching everything, so I went out and got a bike of my own!"

Kasey's first bike was a Honda 500-4; one that she first had trouble turning around in her own cul-de-sac. She started learning how to ride on a regular motocross track alongside a bunch of teenage boys, and in no time at all, was learning the "lingo"... phrases like "dump your clutch"; which, in layman's terms means "put it in gear." "Grab a handful" was when you'd "grab the handle and twist the accelerator," and as Kasey would add, "You'd haul ass!"

By Christmas, she treated herself to a 125cc dirt bike, and in 1972 began doing some serious racing of her own.

It was also around this time that Kasey began writing a column for *Modern Cycle Magazine* called "Powder-Puff," as well as a motorcycling column for the now defunct *Los Angeles Herald Examiner*. Kasey remembered, "I had to be very careful. The article had to be a certain number of words. It would stop right where they said it would. So if your article came in just one word too long…"

She loved every minute of it, and had a great story she liked to tell. "One day I was practicing out on the track, wearing white leathers, a white jersey, white helmet, and black boots. And no chest protector! We didn't have them like they do now… And this big bike came up behind me revving its engine. So I let it go around, and then the rider really pissed me off because he gassed it, and I started getting pelted by all these rocks! So I finished my lap, pulled off the track, and took off my helmet so I could catch my breath.

All of a sudden, the rider of the bike that shot around me drove up, pulled off his helmet, and said, "Kasey!! Oh my God! I didn't know it was a girl. I didn't know it was *you*!" That driver was Steve McQueen!"

Kasey and Steve knew each other because they had worked together a few times on his TV show, *Wanted: Dead or Alive*, and had recently gotten re-acquainted around the track, as Steve was one great racer, and had two kids that used to race with Mike.

Kasey loved that story, but the "girl" comment always stuck in her craw. She felt that girls could race just as well as guys, and should be taken more seriously in the sport.

By 1974, Kasey proved just that by establishing the PURR (Powder-Puffs Unlimited Riders and Racers) Association and later that same year, the first Powder-Puff National.

A year later, she approached the promoter of "the Superbowl of Motocross" to allow ten of the top women in racing to compete in a Women's Invitational Trophy Dash. The man agreed and the event was a huge success, having been witnessed by some 80,000 spectators in the Los Angeles Coliseum. And one photo in particular of Sue Fish, wearing a halter top and leathers astride her bike went "viral" in a 1970s sort of way putting the event and women in moto-cross on the map!

Kasey also planned and organized the International Women's Motorcycle Championship, a successful race that boasted over 350 women from all over the United States.

I always relished listening to Kasey when she talked about her Motocross days because you could see the excitement and passion in her eyes—much more than when she'd talk about her film and TV career.

Every now and then, we used to go down to the Glen Helen Race Track when they were having motocross races and I'd practically have to hold her in her seat because she wanted to get back out there on a bike!

Kasey was a monumental pioneer in the world of Women's Motocross Racing, and of all of her accomplishments, whether it was working with the big names of the day like Alfred Hitchcock and Frank Capra, or starring in two of the most successful television series ever made, motocross racing was her most beloved accomplishment.

Chapter 8
MY BIG MOVE

In February of 1992, Kasey came to Atlanta to conduct an actor's workshop that I helped set up with local friends and actors. Instead of staying at the hotel where the class would be held, she ended up staying at home with my parents and me. Mom and Dad loved Kasey and the feeling was mutual. To say we had a blast was putting it mildly.

Finally, one night before heading back to L.A., we were sitting in my Dad's car and after an hour of chatting, Kasey looked at me and said, "Mark, if you ever want to get this *Bewitched... Again!* thing off the ground, you need to be in Hollywood."

"But I can't afford to be in Hollywood," I replied.

"Well, come and stay with me for a couple of weeks."

Needless to say, that was all the invitation I needed.

On March 8th, 1992, I arrived in Los Angeles

Two days later I picked up a harried Kasey at LAX. She had been on another teaching gig in Texas that had been a huge bust. She badly needed some cheering up, so we went out to dinner and then home.

I never left.

And there you have the title of this book: The Fan Who Came to Dinner!

Go ahead, turn the book on end! You have never seen such a magical line-up in one photo! This was taken in June of 1968 as the Stars of Screen Gems got off the plane in Mexico City for a Junket that Kasey and her then husband Bud Lewis hosted for all the shows of ABC. L-R: Vito Scotti, David White, Sally Field, Barbara Eden, Alejandro Rey, Hayden Roarke, Agnes Moorehead, Macdonald Carey. Also present was the cast of Here Come the Brides, Screen Gems president, Jackie Cooper and many others. Elizabeth Montgomery and husband Bill Asher did NOT attend as their relations with ABC and Jackie Cooper were always a bit off.

Chapter 9
WINK

This was taken in the lobby of the famed Ravenswood Apartments. It was here that Mae West lived most of her adult life.

Kasey had a dog named Wink. Wink was a tiny, white Maltese who had a Napoleon complex… as he loved to pick on anything bigger than himself and often did. Wink's thinking was that he could win any fight. The other dog's was "Hors d'oeuvres"!

I had never had a dog before I inherited Wink. Winker. Winkmeister. Winkums. You name it, that's what we called him!

I was so blessed. This dog worshiped the water he thought I walked on and I loved that little guy with all my heart.

Kasey used to joke that before I arrived, Wink had been *her* dog, because the very first night I was in the condo, he jumped off her bed, ran into my room, and never went back! That dog and I were as inseparable as Kasey and I had become. My first ever dog!

Within days of my moving in, I remember noticing little droppings between the dresser and chest of drawers in my room that certainly couldn't be Wink's, and it was then I realized we had a little "visitor" running around! Kasey and I went to the store and bought one of those tiny mouse traps to set out. That night, I remember telling her, "If I hear that thing go off, I'm coming to get you no matter what time it is!"

About 1:30 AM I awoke to a "snap." I lay there thinking, "I'm not going to wake her up… I am NOT going to wake her…" I couldn't stand it. I went to get her. KR quickly grabbed a brown paper grocery bag and a yard stick to scoop up *the remains*. Slowly, we peered between the two pieces of furniture.

There was the trap.

There was the cheese.

But there was no mouse.

However, as we both slowly turned our heads, there, under a small rocking chair in my room, lay the biggest RAT you've ever seen! (No kidding at least 18" from tip to tail!!!)

Moving? *Nope.*

Dead? *Who knew?*

Kasey slowly pushed the chair. The rudder of the rocker tapped it, but it still didn't move.

So, bag in hand, Kasey and I moved closer. She was going to flip it into the bag with the yard stick.

The very moment she touched it, that damn thing took off like a shot and flew down an open hole in *my* wall where a cable switch plate was missing.

Now, imagine if you will those old *Tom and Jerry* cartoons where the lady sees the mouse and jumps up on a chair holding her skirt around her thighs, and begins screaming at the top of her lungs.

Yeah, sad to say, that was me!

Finally, we stuffed the hole with a plastic bag and put packing tape to cover it but all through the night, I could hear the crunching of little teeth on plastic!

That April, only a month into my new life, Kasey and I made contact with former *Bewitched* stars Erin Murphy, Dick Sargent, and Sandra Gould. We held an impromptu *Bewitched* Reunion in Kasey's acting studio, The Hollywood Underground Network in North Hollywood, which once sat on Weddington Street, right next to the Academy of Television Arts and Sciences. In recent years it has been demolished to make way for more apartments, condos, and a railway station.

It was a great little reunion! We played a video about *Bewitched... Again!* that I had made in Atlanta with me playing Adam. Afterwards, I was highly praised by all. Talk about walking on air! AND, all said they would be right in there pitching with us to get the new series idea on air! I have no photos from this BUT recently I found a video that captured a short burst of this momentous occasion, and I am so glad that I have it.

Kasey and I soon began visiting all the "touristy" places together. On our first evening in Hollywood we parked the car right next to Snow White's star on Hollywood Boulevard. (A cartoon character received her own star, yet it took seventeen more years to get one for Elizabeth Montgomery?!)

We ventured to the Renaissance Faire, Calico Ghost Town (a manufactured town that used real buildings from the Old West), and Universal Studios. I remember on one of our many trips there, we went on the Jurassic Park ride, which was new at the time. We sat in the front as planned because on the big drop, you can duck and all the water gets splashed on the guy behind you!

Unfortunately, all that planning proved futile as Kasey froze and forgot to duck!

When I looked up, I saw that her entire face had been washed clean and her hair was drenched! But always the good sport, she just went to the ladies room and blew herself dry with the hand drier!

One passion of mine was to visit all the different cemeteries and take my photo with ALL of the famous dead people I could find.

Mark and Bette Davis
Mark and Tyrone Power
Mark and Marilyn Monroe
Mark and L. Frank Baum...

L to R: KR as Elizabeth the First, Me as Sir Walter Raleigh, being boiled in my own bath water at Calico Ghost Town and Kasey after her Jurassic drenching!

We finally made a scrapbook and called it "Mark's Book of the Dead"!

I figured the closest I'd ever get to any of them was six feet *above*... unless of course, they had been interred in a vault!

Which brings me to my next story...

Chapter 10

CLIFTON AND INA

After umpteen trips to several graveyards, we were walking in Hollywood Memorial Park (Today Hollywood Forever. For you *Bewitched* fans, that's where David White has been laid to rest with his son, Jonathan.)

Kasey and I began walking down the hollow aisles of one of the mausoleums in search of Clifton Webb who has been reputed to haunt that cemetery. As I was relating this story to Kasey, our footsteps began echoing off the marbled walls, floors, ceilings, and monuments, and we quickly found it to be a very cold unsettling place. We were a bit spooked, but finally found Clifton in a wall vault about waist high. Kasey told me to hurry and stand beside the vault so she could take the picture and we could get out of there!

I walked over, leaned against the marble piece that had his name on it, and as I did, the wall gave way and landed with a resounding "CLUNK" against his casket! I screamed (again!) and I also ran behind her! I am such the hero! HA!

At any rate, Kasey began snapping pictures like mad, just waiting for the ectoplasm to come seeping out.

We got the photos back and guess what?! NOTHING!

That August, Kasey's mom, Ina, celebrated her 92nd birthday. Ina couldn't remember very much, but she used to smile from ear-to-ear when I'd come into her room at the nursing home. Apparently she had an eye for the "gentleman callers."

Ina, who had been an upstanding member of the Eastern Star organization, and used to throw many formal parties for them, always felt she was in charge at Dryer's Nursing Home in Burbank.

Mr. Webb did not have the decency to show up on film!

For her birthday, Kasey and I planned to pick up Ina and go across the street to meet some other family members at Bob's Big Boy restaurant.

This was all dangerous business because we had to wheel Ina over in her wheel-chair and cross traffic on a busy street. Ina made things all the more difficult because she kept dragging her feet! Finally I popped a wheelie with her in the chair and flew across the busy intersection with Ina screaming all the way… Geeze, I coulda killed us!

Me and Kasey's mom, Ina.

Could it be that McMann and Tate were romancing an account from NASA? Why else would the agency owner's wife, Louise be with Majors Nelson and Healey on a tarmac?

Chapter 11
A Precursor of Things to Come

In late September, Kasey felt a lump on the side of her neck. It proved to be a rather large benign tumor, but the doctors still felt it should be removed if only for precautionary measures. It was located in the parotid gland so they removed it along with most of her thyroid. I can remember being scared, because no one I had ever known had had any surgery. As they wheeled her into the operating room at the Motion Picture Hospital, she made sure to tell me that if anything happened, "Tell my children I love them."

It was all quite nerve wracking!

After she was out of sight, I rushed to the mall where she had recently seen and fallen in love with this big, clay Jack o'Lantern in a coffee shop. I bought it and went back to her hospital room to wait. Luckily, the surgery turned out to be rather simple, and she awoke to this big grinning clay orb staring at her. She loved it.

That woman could heal faster than anybody I've ever known and because of that, our Hallowe'en preparations were still on for that year.

Our first Hallowe'en party was a blast! Kasey wore the pink lamé Victorian gown that I designed and brought with me the previous year (She trusted my costuming ability by this time) and looked like a million bucks!

On Hallowe'en night, we went to Beverly Hills and ran into Milton Berle who was in full drag, completely blitzed, and constantly pulling up his skirt. It was kinda like looking at a train wreck… You don't want to watch but you can't help it… So we wisely decided to go elsewhere!

Kasey's gown had 52 handmade dark pink lamé roses across the top and front and over 100 green lamé leaves. Each flower and leaf was "dotted" with several sequins in the same colors. Matching feather headdress and hot pink boa completed the look! I'm just a devil. HA! 27 years after it was first made, I gave it to my dear friend Roberta.

The St. Nicholas Ball acting like mannequins with our friend Julia!

Christmas that year offered another opportunity to dress-up; the annual St. Nicholas Ball that our dear friend Julia DelJudge chaired every year at the Los Angeles Biltmore Hotel.

It was a lovely affair! Every ballroom was decorated in a different color. One that I especially remember was decorated with a live tree that reached all the way to the ceiling, completely dressed in Tiffany ornaments!

The stipulation for the ball was that you had to dress Victorian. Of course the Victorian era offered up several different dress styles, so Kasey wore a huge red and black lace hoop dress of the Civil War period that I had made a few years earlier.

There was just one problem… she couldn't get in the car while wearing it! So when it was time to leave the ball, the valet brought the car around and I stepped behind Kasey, pulled two draw strings simultaneously, and down came the huge skirt and hoop. She casually stepped out of it wearing nothing but the top, her feathers, and a pair of black leggings! The poor valet stood there mortified, having just seen this gracious lady drop her dress in public!

After picking it up and stuffing it in the trunk, I tipped the valet and off we drove, laughing the whole way home.

Chapter 12
SON OF A WITCH

1993 was a fun year! My sister was married on the 30th of January, 1993, and I was asked to sing at her wedding (I had been a night club singer for years back in Georgia). I remember the day was cold and rainy and there were a billion crows on the lawn of the church. Odd the things you remember... But Kate, my sister, looked beautiful!

During that time, I also began training to be a tour guide at Universal Studios. It was such a kick getting to *play* in the back-lot on all those famous exteriors and sets—The Munster's House, The Psycho House and the Bates Motel, The Chicken Ranch, and the New York Street where *The Sting* was filmed.

But that situation didn't last long when I found out that in order to get you to work there, they lure you with the possibilities of getting to meet the big names in show business, and then after graduating (I was one of only nine that made it out of thirty) it really doesn't pan out that way. They never intended to give us a chance to work with the big names. They used that as a come-on. It's as if they train you and then say, "Just kidding!"

I did have a fun time doing my first musical in California that year. The show was *Carousel* and I played Enoch Snow. Actually I played him the way I thought Jim Carry would. (Isn't that what musical comedy is for?!) The audience laughed but the director didn't... sigh, why does genius always go un-rewarded?! HA!

Kasey and I also attended her 50th High School reunion that year in Burbank. Looking back, it was kind of funny. Kasey, being the only one in her class to go into show business, showed up with her "boy-toy" on her arm! We never thought anything about it, but we found out during the course of the evening that's exactly what everyone was thinking!

Publicity still for our script Son of A Witch (NOT to be confused with *Bewitched... Again!*). The "Alligator Bag" was going to have vicious looking teeth put into its mouth as it was not supposed to like "Elliott" (Kasey)!

Me at the famous *Munster's House* while preparing to be a Universal Tour Guide.

We also visited the Museum of Natural History in Los Angeles that year. Kasey and I walked over to where a bunch of kids had gathered. They were looking at the remains of a 4000 year old mummy that was on display and partially unwrapped.

"I remember this from when I was a kid," she said. I immediately quipped, "Don't be silly, he wasn't dead yet!" If it hadn't been so funny she may have killed me on the spot!

While there we were scouting locations for our new witch story this time around called *Son of a Witch*!

With all the copyright troubles we were having with the *Bewitched* franchise, we decided to write a brand new story about America's first boy-witch and take it completely out of the copy-written world of Samantha Stephens.

The story was a good one too, if I do say so myself. A combination of *Superman* meets *Cinderella* meets *Bewitched*. *Son of a Witch* is the story of Sam Haines (anyone get that joke?), a baby who is sent to the future from the persecuted 1690s of Salem, Massachusetts by his doomed-to-die witch parents, and grows up in a Catholic orphanage totally unaware of his "heretical heritage."

Enter three elderly witches from his past; Edna, Mrs. Gladstone, and Tituba, who witnessed his transport to the future, and who have been trying to find him for centuries. As they soon find out, he's actually been under their very noses the entire time, but having never practiced any spells, they were unable to see him in the crystal ball.

With the help of his "familiar," an alligator bag (see picture) he was placed in as a baby, they find him and implore him to sign an official Son-of-A-Witch contract before all hell breaks loose at midnight on Halloween, his 31st birthday. It's a fun story with a lot of humor and Sam even saves the day in the end by twitching his nose, to which the other witches ask "Where did you learn that?"

"Reruns!"

Son of a Witch would have boasted quite a memorable cast. Mrs. Gladstone was to be played by Sandra Gould. Bernard Fox would play Professor Hawthorne, a modern day witch hunter (whose daughter, Judy, Sam is engaged to), and Marla Gibbs would rule the roost as the rather imposing witch Tituba.

Rose Marie would round out the cast as the Reverend Mother (bow well hidden under habit).

Sam would teach grade school history, paving the way for kids to be introduced to the episodes, greatly adding to the fun as they help the witches convince Sam about his past.

Kathleen Freeman, the doddering witch, Edna, would be computer proficient and cast spells by looking them up under "spell check".

Unfortunately, the project was never given the green light, so one can only imagine what a fun show that would have been.

During this same time, the Internet began to pick up steam, Kasey and I happened upon one of the first web sites about *Bewitched*; one sponsored by Nick-at-Nite. Kasey was fascinated by its potential, so we immediately began *surfing* the web.

I certainly can't blame them, but most Nick-at-Nite fans wouldn't believe that it was actually KASEY ROGERS answering their questions on the *Bewitched* message board. A few of them got downright mean-spirited about it, thinking someone was pulling their leg, but we just used to laugh. So if any of you doubters are reading this, and I hope you are, guess what?! That really was "Louise Tate"!

We actually met a few of those fans, first from the Nick-at-Nite site, and later from a website run by our soon-to-be-dear friends, Joe and Wendy. Some of these fans, including Joe, even flew out to attend our *infamous* Halloween parties. If you look at Joe and Wendy's site on www.bewitched.net, you can still find many pictures from those halcyon days of Hallowe'en.

Chapter 13

Witches in Clouds, Monsters in Trees; Happy Times with Mark and KR

Yes, silly title.

Kasey and I had the uncanny knack of being able to "see" the exact same figures in clouds. It's funny—we would see witches on brooms all the time! At the beach, at dinner, in the leaves of a tree by the lake across the street, and once even in a cloud at her brother's house on Thanksgiving! We got everyone to see that one!

But it didn't stop there.

Often we'd pass two very distinctive looking trees. One looked like a monster on its hind legs holding a rag doll and another looked like an angel's wing open for flight. (Even Sandy Gould once saw that one!)

Clouds and trees weren't the only things we could "see" things in. We were also pretty good with puddles!

The things we'd "see" in puddles usually made us laugh because invariably, they were "dirty" pictures. We even began shooting photos of our finds and wanted to put a book together called "Pornographic Puddles," but we never did. (In the attempt of keeping this book rated "G," I won't be including any of those photos!) Speaking of visceral subjects:

OK, so if you ever wanted proof positive that Endora really, REALLY liked the food at Mario's, here it is! Agnes Moorehead boogies the night away with Vito Scotti.

Chapter 14
The Poop Deck

Once when Kasey and I were getting ready to go somewhere, I needed to let Wink out so he could go to the back deck (forever christened "The Poop Deck"). The sliding glass door in my room was temperamental and too hard to lock and un-lock, so sometimes I would use Kasey's bedroom single door to let him in and out. I knocked on Kasey's door and asked if she was decent.

She quickly answered, "Yes," so I opened the door.

There she was in all her glory, bent over with her pants around her ankles!

Full moon. Starless night!

The moment hung like hours as I slowly, silently, closed the door.

She busted out laughing and I was immediately on the floor in hysterics trying to spit out, "You said you were decent!!!" I guess she didn't expect me to really open the door, but we laughed about it for years, just as we did this one.

On the "Poop Deck" there once sat a curved wrought iron chair with no cushion. In the middle of the night, Kasey arose to go to the bathroom. She really wasn't prone to sleep-walking but somehow she managed to unlock her door, go outside, sit down on the wrought iron chair and "commence," before she woke up and realized what she was doing!

The next morning through tears of laughter, she confessed to me what had happened. There she sat staring at me asleep through the sliding glass door and silently praying, "Oh Mark, please don't wake up! Please don't wake up!"

Luckily, for her sake, I didn't, but *boy howdee*, I'm still getting mileage out of that story!

As you can tell, you never knew what Kasey was going to do.

She once told me that she and her second husband, Bud Lewis, attended a sort of "garage sale" at the Ambassador Hotel, where Bobby Kennedy was killed, shortly before it closed down.

She ended up buying a couple of tall candles, but later got rid of them after they began to lose their shape. The other thing she ended up nabbing that day from the hotel was one of the bullet holes from the kitchen wall! She actually snuck into the kitchen where that unfortunate event had taken place on June 5th, 1968, and gouged out one of the bullet holes made by Kennedy's assassin, Sirhan Sirhan! I still have it somewhere in a baggie, along with a chip off of L. Frank Baum's tombstone that I picked up on one of our cemetery adventures.

Chapter 15
Earthquake '94

Sounds like the name of one of those disaster movies from the past, but guess what? It *was* a disaster and it all began precisely at 4:32 a.m. on Monday, January 17th, forever known as the day Northridge fell down!

The room was pulsating back and forth! I remember leaping out of bed and losing my balance as I came to the little hallway that separated my room and bathroom from the rest of the condo. I was yelling for Kasey, but she wasn't answering. It never occurred to me she couldn't hear me over the roar. I hadn't a clue where Wink was, as he had been on the bed next to me.

I was momentarily trapped inside the hallway. Eerily, it was still dark outside, yet everything was bathed in blue light, reminiscent of a full moon. I grabbed the first available door knob I could find and ended up back in my bedroom!

When the first quake subsided, I found Kasey out in the kitchen. I began feeling nauseous and ended up lying down on the floor with my feet up. As I did, I could hear glass crunching underneath my back. There was broken glass everywhere. It's amazing I didn't get cut.

I quickly recovered and Kasey handed me a paper bag and the two of us spent the next few hours amidst tremendous aftershocks throwing away anything that had once been made of glass.

Luckily, I had the foresight to quickly call my Mom and Dad down in Atlanta. They were not up yet, but I had enough time to tell them no matter what they heard on the news, Kasey and I were fine. It would be days before we would be able to make any more calls in or out.

A couple of odd incidents also happened that day. Kasey had two, rather stylized glass swans with long thin necks that sat on small bases about the size of a quarter. They were heavy enough to keep them from falling over, but had moved all the way to the edge of the table. Just one more inch and we would have added them to that paper bag.

Kasey also had a small plant still sitting in its same spot on a dresser in her bedroom that was completely missing its pot. It was days before we came to the conclusion that the plant must've leapt into the air, just as the drawer opened, swallowing the pot, and then closing again as the plant came back down right into place!

I had a small picture of Kasey and me at the Christmas ball we attended in '92 on my chest of drawers, but it was nowhere to be found.

It was *years* later, as I was moving furniture out of the room to paint it, I found that same picture *embedded* in the wall, with only about a half inch of it sticking out!

My favorite line through all of this?

"I promise NEVER to try that spell again!!!"

Grauman's *Egyptian* Theatre, a national landmark in Hollywood, was heavily damaged during the rumble. It had been the site of the first-ever Hollywood premiere in 1925, complete with dancing slave girls and Roman soldiers standing on parapets with pots that shot flames into the air. The film was Robin Hood starring Douglas Fairbanks Sr.

Kasey and I got one of our wild hairs about starting a campaign to have it restored, but someone else had already beaten us to the punch. We didn't care as long as something was being done.

But before we knew that, Kasey and I were looking around the outside of the Egyptian, when she noticed that the back door was ajar. She went in and I panicked! But follow, I must!

It was incredibly dark, except for some brilliant shafts of light entering the room at all angles from the holes in the back wall where the screen had once hung. This is where Myrna Loy once worked as a hat check girl.

We stepped over a sleeping bum and wound our way up to the entrance of the theatre. From our clandestine spot, we noticed a security guard in the forecourt, who had no idea intruders were watching from within! Kasey and I quickly picked up the fragments from the head of a toppled plaster Egyptian sentry and quietly snuck back out. I still have the pieces somewhere in a box buried deep in storage, as one day I want to have them restored and mounted, as if it were some priceless, ancient relic. Because of its history, in many ways to me, it is.

Kasey and I shared an affinity for Hollywood landmarks. In the middle of Hollywood, there once stood an incredible edifice known as The Garden of Allah. It stood on the grounds of the home of silent film star Alla Nazimova! She later turned her palatial home into a hotel by building discreet bungalows all about her property. It sat at the corner of Crescent Heights and the legendary Sunset Boulevard, just across the street from where the famed Schwab's Drug Store once stood. Today, what sits there? A bank and a McDonald's... sad.

In August, 1959, when this iconic palace closed its doors for the last time, Kasey and Bud went trudging through the gardens where she snipped a piece of a jade plant.

Kasey always enjoyed the odd habit of *wild-flower picking*! What that actually means is if she saw a flower or plant growing in someone's yard, she'd pluck it right out, roots and all! She LOVED to root plants in cups and then plant them on the front porch in one of a myriad of pots.

That same jade plant that Kasey plucked from the Garden of Allah all those years ago somehow survived the test of time and grew into a small behemoth on the front porch of our condo.

We always talked about selling clippings of it with a picture of the infamous landmark it came from, but that's another business venture that only made it into the talking stage.

Believe it or not, I still have it happily growing where I live now.

1994 was also the year that I met my dear friend, SueAne Langdon.

Years before, I had once performed Elvis' version of Frankie & Johnny at a theme park in Atlanta. There was one girl in the cast who played the character of "Mitzi," which had been originated by SueAne in the movie with Elvis Presley.

In the song, Mitzi (SueAne) tells Frankie that Johnnie is two-timing her with Nellie Blye. "Frankie! I don't wanna make you no trouble! *Honey*, I don't wanna tell you no lies!"

Me and SueAne Langdon at a Stagecoach Inn Museum Halloween benefit in 2005.

Needless to say, "*Honey*" became our catch phrase around the park. We would constantly yell it at each other! All those years later, here I stood reciting those memories to the original actress who played Mitzi in *Frankie and Johnnie*: SueAne Langdon.

It wasn't long before we all became fast friends—SueAne, her husband Jack, Kasey, and me. Sometimes Sue would call the house phone and just leave a one word message on the answering machine... "Honey!"

As I said at the beginning of the book, I will always treasure SueAne's friendship. Here's to ya, "Honey!"

Chapter 16
I Went to the Circus with Gladys Kravitz

Me taking a picture of Sandy in her backyard on what we *later found out* was her 80th birthday July 23rd 1996.

I always thought THAT would make a great title for my biography. And we did actually go to the circus together.

Kasey, Sandy, and I attended an autograph signing show in San Jose`, California on September 7th and 8th of 1996 where we were nicely wined and dined. But after arriving early on our first evening there, we found we had nothing to do. So we decided to take a walk around the hotel.

During our sojourn, we happened to spot a flyer that announced the Ringling Bros. and Barnum and Bailey Circus was in town, only blocks away from our hotel.

We spent an enjoyable evening eating peanuts and popcorn while watching the trained horses, elephants, and all of the other amazing animal acts. Of course, no circus would be complete without the clowns, but Barnum and Bailey had nothing on us that night. The biggest attraction at the circus that evening was in the bleachers right beside Kasey and me... Sandra "Gladys" Gould.

Anyone who knew her would tell you that Sandra loved to be the center of attention by making sure that everyone knew she was there. More than once, Kasey had been mortified by Sandra's announcement to unknown women in a ladies room: "We're from *Bewitched*!" And that's how it was that evening at the circus; Sandra making sure that everyone knew she was there, and happily signed autographs all evening. Sandra Gould commanded the center ring at all times.

A lot of people ask me what "Mrs. Kravitz" was really like. To be honest, she was sometimes a hard lady and definitely a force to be reckoned with, because what you *saw* was what you *got* with Sandra.

She was loud, shrill, and boisterous. She entered the room as "Gladys Kravitz" and would yell "Abner!!" at the drop of a hat for anyone that would listen. I don't know if that was something she always did, or just developed that persona over the years because it was expected of her, but when I met her, it WAS her.

With that being said, she was also lots and lots of FUN! She had a heart of gold and would do anything for you and often did! She was always laughing and had more fun living life than anyone I've ever known.

In 1997, my birthday fell on Easter Sunday and Sandy gave a huge party in my honor. Kasey, Bernard and Jacque Fox, Marla Gibbs, and many others were guests along with my Mom and Dad who were visiting from Georgia.

Also at the party was one of Sandy's closest friends, Teddy Getty who was quite a character herself.

Teddy Getty at one time had been married to the famous J. Paul, and once as an American opera star in Germany during World War II, she had been accused of being a spy. J. Paul somehow managed to step in and save her from being executed.

Unfortunately, they would later divorce after the death of their son, because J. Paul wouldn't fly home from a business trip to be

Chapter 16: I Went to the Circus with Gladys Kravitz

L-R Me, Pete Trujillo, Marla Gibbs, Sandy. Pete worked for the *Globe* (yep, a *scandal rag*!) and we adored him. He died much too young from weight related heart issues. Marla Gibbs is incredible... so funny and yet soft spoken in reality.

with them as the boy's death became inevitable. If that seems a little heartless, consider that in 1973, his grandson, J. Paul Getty the 3rd, was kidnapped in Italy and his kidnappers sent them one of his ears and demanded a $16 million-dollar ransom. It's reported that J. Paul initially balked about paying up and reportedly said, "I have fourteen other grandchildren. If I pay one penny now, then I'll have fourteen kidnapped grandchildren." Eventually over $2 million was paid by the Getty family and the grandson was released, though no one is quite sure just how much money J. Paul the 1st contributed.

Later in life, Teddy began a business venture bottling water from a little town in Texas called "The Town without a Toothache" because the water was so high in fluoride.

Me and Teddy Getty!

After that, she began making candy in her garage that sold for many years in the upper end stores of Los Angeles.

As you can tell, Teddy Getty's adventures could fill a book all her own.

FUN NOTE: Teddy Getty was the owner of "Norma Desmond's" mansion used in the movie *Sunset Boulevard*. It originally stood on the corner of Wilshire and Crenshaw Boulevards in Los Angeles, and had been passed on to her in the divorce settlement from J. Paul. She in turn, rented it out to Paramount to be used in the film on the condition that Paramount build her a swimming pool, which they did, and can be seen in the final production.

Sadly, the mansion was torn down in 1957 to make way for Getty Headquarters. Today it is known as the Harbor Building.

Sandra loved to cook and Kasey and I were invited over to her house for many parties through the years. She considered herself quite the gourmet and I was the ONLY one she ever allowed in her kitchen. She always talked about writing a cookbook called "*Sex, Pots, and Pans: How to Cook for Every Kind of Man!*" She wanted to include recipes from all the glamour girls in Hollywood. (Some bio's written about Sandra state that this book was actually written, but to my knowledge it never was.)

Long before *Bewitched*, she *did* write a book called "*Always Say Maybe*" which can sometimes be found on eBay. She also made a record called "Melvin, This is Mother." It was the flip side to the old hit, "Hello Muddah, Hello Faddah." These are fun collectibles and I urge any fan to try their luck at finding these forgotten treasures.

At the time of her death, Sandy had been working on another book called "*Confessions of a Hollywood Voyeur.*" It was to be a collection of semi-dirty stories about the many celebrities she had known throughout the years. For some reason, she loved to relate stories that were literally "below-the-belt." One in particular I remember was the time that Sandra's husband invited actor Forrest Tucker (*F-Troop, Auntie Mame*) over for dinner. Apparently, it was pretty common knowledge around Tinsel Town that Forrest was significantly endowed, but according to Sandra, it was her husband who informed her of Forrest and his "friend." (I've always wondered how her husband knew…) When Forrest arrived for dinner, Sandra greeted him at the door and said, "How are you, Forrest?" And then, looking directly at his fly said, "And how are *you*?!" I'm not sure how far she had gotten on the project or what became of the work she had finished, but can you imagine what a read that would have been?!

Sandy had a great house and lived right off Laurel Canyon Blvd, which is a main thoroughfare from the Valley to Hollywood. You'd enter her home through a double front door into a little foyer with a huge black lacquer Oriental cabinet. Straight ahead, two steps up, was the dining room table. The entire room was the color of a ripe watermelon.

Off to the right of the dining room was the kitchen. The living room, off to the right of the foyer, was separated by a free standing fireplace. Then up a couple more steps was a den that led out to the pool.

One of Sandra's guest rooms doubled as an office and had a sign on it that said "Caution, Baby Lion Sleeping!" Also in her office was a word processor that she had never taken out of the box, as she preferred the old fashioned world of her electric typewriter. She hated computers and would always say: "I don't want anything *on* when *I'm* not!"

Sandra always kept plenty of hand written notes around, and one day when I was organizing her office, I discovered that some of these hand written notes were on the *backs* of old *Bewitched* scripts! I was absolutely mortified! She could have cared less and asked me if I wanted them... What do you think I said??? Unfortunately by that time, the only two scripts that were still salvageable were *Mary the Good Fairy* and *Weep No More My Willow*. (I made sure that she and Bernard Fox signed that one!)

One memorable evening, we were getting things ready for a dinner party when I noticed ANTS had made their way in and were crawling all over the kitchen counters and sink. Worrying that guests would be arriving any minute, I yelled, "Sandra, there are ants all over the place!" Not the least bit concerned, she said, "Those aren't ants. That's just pepper!" To which I replied, "Pepper doesn't crawl through the sink!" Almost immediately guests began arriving, so all we could do was laugh... and squash!

Another occasion she allowed me in her kitchen was at a Labor Day cookout in 1996. She had a pot of plump hot dogs boiling on the stove, and every few minutes she would run over, stab one with a fork, pull it out, and wave it around while hollering, "Nobody I know!" "Nobody I know!"

Chapter 16: I Went to the Circus with Gladys Kravitz

"Nobody I know!"

Several times, Sandy wanted my help with a bit of redecorating. She needed a bookcase in her living room, so we decided to enclose the left side of her free-standing fireplace, which was only about two feet wide. This little project turned out great and it made a great open bookcase for her many "tchochkes."

Sandra Gould circa 1950s.

Chapter 16: I Went to the Circus with Gladys Kravitz

Sandra and husband, Hollingsworth Morse.

Once I made her a shower curtain out of some fabric we happened upon that exactly matched her bathroom wallpaper. Another one of our projects included building an "L" shaped storage bench under two windows in her bedroom. It turned out nicely, but oh that bedroom!! She must've had THIRTY YEARS worth of National Geographic Magazines stacked up in the corner. The sad thing is that when we tried to get rid of them, no school—no library—no one wanted them, so we ended up just throwing them out.

Every year, Sandra would come to our Hallowe'en parties at the condo. She had an incredible memory, noticing the smallest of details. If something wasn't in the exact spot it was in at the previous year's party, she'd ask me about it!

She was a whiz at remembering names, and when she met someone new at our parties, she had a knack of getting their life story out of them in ten minutes, and would always remember it when she ran into them again! "Oh, you're Alex from Texas!"

Sandra liked to know *everything* that was going on and constantly insisted that Bernard Fox tell her how much he made at the autograph shows they all did together. It really got her goose, because he'd never tell!

With first husband CBS exec Larry Berns gone, Sandra was happily married for the second time to director Hollingsworth Morse. If the name sounds familiar, you've probably seen it on countless TV credits throughout the years; *Lassie, Marcus Welby M.D., The Dukes of Hazzard, The Fall Guy,* etc. And for those of us that remember Saturday morning TV, his name can also be found on the credits of *H.R. Pufnstuf, Isis,* and *Shazam!*

Kasey was always proud of the fact that she had played a small part in getting them together. One day on the *Bewitched* set, Sandra was chit-chatting with Kasey in between scenes. Sandra told her, "I don't know what to do. Hollingsworth Morse has been pursuing me, is very interested in me, and has asked me to marry him. I just don't know what to do!" Kasey immediately said, "MARRY HIM!"

So she did!

Hanging in the middle of their home was a huge oil painting of Freddie the Flute from *H.R. Pufnstuf,* with a mat signed by all the people on the show.

Sandra, also a fantastic artist, had many of her own paintings hanging throughout the house. One I remember in particular was a colorful carnival scene she painted from the actual carnival used in an episode of *Bewitched* called "*Tabitha's Very Own Samantha.*"

The day after the '94 earthquake, Kasey and I called Sandy to see if she was alright. She laughed and said everything was alright with the exception of a pot of spaghetti that had been cooking on the stove and was now all over the ceiling, counters, and floor. I have to admire her. There she was standing with noodles hanging down over her head, but she was still able to laugh about it.

Bewitched fans will find this fun. Sandy's kitchen stove was the exact model used on the show; a Frigidaire Flair, complete with burners on a sliding drawer that could be pulled out and pushed back in. She loved it so much from the show that she went out and bought herself one just like it!

Sandy decided that she needed to redecorate her kitchen. She hired a guy named Ralph to do most of the work. Ralph had no front teeth, but was a lot of fun. One day I was over helping Sandra clean out the pantry. I was digging through all the jars, cans, and boxes when I unearthed a jar of Cheeze-Whiz, which is usually bright orange. Well, not *this* jar! It had turned to moldy *gray.* Then

Oil painting of Freddy the Flute from *H.R. Pufinstuf*. I wish you could see the "mod" colors of this.

I noticed an expiration date of 1974 (20 years!)! Needless to say, that unearthed treasure went right in the garbage.

Continuing to dig through all the clutter, I discovered a tin of Oreo cookies that I later found out had been given to her by Joan Rivers as a present for being on her show. When I opened up the tin, I found a mound of half-eaten cookies entirely covered in *webs*! It was *completely* webbed over! That got tossed too.

Also in Sandra's pantry were cans of *corn*. There had to be at least FORTY of them and most of them were bulging! She was working

I don't have a picture of that (DAMN!) but here's one of Sandy and Kasey in the pool that day!

in another part of the house, so every time I would come across another can of corn, I'd yell "CORN!" Then Ralph would yell "CORN!" and then Sandra would chime in from way down the hall, "CORN!!" I sometimes think if I'd kept digging, I might've found Jimmy Hoffa… there was never a dull moment with "Mrs. Kravitz"! I miss her so very, very much.

This is neat: On the top of Sandra's refrigerator sat the cake topper from her wedding to "Holly." It still had the now brown frosting caked around the plastic bottom. Even the bride and grooms feet had frosting remnants on it. I remember meticulously cleaning the frosting off so that it could be put back on top of the fridge. It still had the original price tag, $1.39, on the bottom. Many years later, long after Sandy had gone, I was in a thrift store with my friend Darlene near her house. Honest to God there it sat. I bought it and still have it!

In August of '97, we were having a pool party at our friend Scott Awley's. Sandy attended and changed her clothes, putting on a black sundress that she wore to get in the pool. Suddenly I realized a chance of a life time… So I snuck into Scott's spare room, put Sandra's panties on my head and fastened her bra around my chest. Then I sauntered out to the pool…

If you thought Sandra could scream "Abner!" you haven't *lived* until you've heard her scream "MAAAAAAAARRRRRK!!!"

Once I accompanied Sandy to the Comedy Awards and got to meet Jim Carrey and Tom Hanks! I also was NOT prepared to go and being last minute I ended up wearing one of Holly's old sport coats and my jeans to a formal affair! Sandy made up a silly story that I had just flown in and the airlines lost my luggage! Yet another time, she coerced me into accompanying a young lady-friend of hers to the Thalian's Ball.

It seems this gal's date had cancelled on her that very day, and she called Sandy in a panic. I was at her house at the time and Sandy told her, "Don't worry! I have someone for you!" (She didn't even ask, although I would've gone anyway.) Again, the only trouble was I had no tuxedo and had to go in a suit and tie. Kathryn, the young lady I escorted, was dressed like "Columbia" from the Rocky Horror Picture Show: sequined jacket, leotard top, and bow tie. It was a very strange evening, but I did meet Michael Feinstein and Liza that night.

At one point, while waiting outside the restrooms for Kathryn, I found myself standing next to Jayne Meadows who was impatiently waiting for her husband, Steve Allen. Suddenly, BOTH Gabor sisters (Zsa-Zsa and Eva) came out of the ladies room bitching at each other up one side and down the other, until they noticed that others were watching. Abruptly they stopped, acted as if nothing happened and skipped off together into the ball room.

A few other *Bewitched* memories from Sandra include the Hallowe'en episode where she was sharing a scene with a goat in the Stephen's kitchen ("The Safe and Sane Hallowe'en"). The goat's actual name was "Louise" (!) and took quite a liking to her.

Sometime later, Sandra did an episode of *The Brady Bunch* ("Getting Greg's Goat") and that *same* goat was on the set and still kept following her around, even to the restroom! In fact, the goat would follow her right into the stall!

And here, I'd like to set the record straight about something... If anyone reading this ever saw the interview Kasey and I gave at the time of Sandra's death to The Globe, we were NOT, as stated in the article, all gathered around her bedside as she passed into the great beyond.

"To Mark, darling, the talented *Bewitched* fan who I love." Love you to, Sandy, so much.

What really happened was that our dear friend Pete Trujillo once worked for that tabloid and wanted to make sure Sandy's passing was duly noted. Unfortunately, the only way they would mention it was if the situation was made it into this epic demise, so the article was greatly dramatized. Sadly, Pete is no longer with us either. He passed away in his early thirties just months before Kasey.

One last Sandy story… One evening she and I were coming home from a shopping trip and were both very hungry. So instead of going out to dinner, she offered to make us something at her home, (steak and peas) and we ate at the small kitchen table that sat next to the door to the backyard and pool.

I mostly remember how her home seemed dark and quite lonesome without the usual crowd and I really sensed that Sandy was very lonesome.

That might explain why she never missed an opportunity to put on her sequins and feathers and go out to what she referred to as the "Disease-of-the-Week" ball.

She was constantly on the go until the very end when God came calling on July 20th, 1999.

Chapter 17
SAMANTHA, JEANNIE, AND JERRY SPRINGER

Some odd things happened in 1995. I went to the funeral of "Samantha," met "Jeannie" (Barbara Eden) for the first time, and flew to Chicago to appear on *The Jerry Springer Show*. This was also the year that Kasey experienced her first bout with cancer.

Elizabeth Montgomery had passed away very suddenly of colorectal cancer on May 18 th. On June 18th, a month to the day, we were invited to attend her memorial service at the Canon Theatre in Beverly Hills. Kasey and I attended with Sandra Gould.

The service was quite touching, and one of my strongest memories of that day was how much Elizabeth's daughter, Rebecca, was so moved by the events. I have since met Rebecca on many happier occasions. Typically, Sandy, quipped afterwards that no one had had the decency to sing Ding Dong the Witch is Dead... I know, I know, rude but funny!

In October of that same year, I attended a play in Long Beach that Barbara Eden was starring in called *Night Club Confidential*. It wasn't until then that I realized how well she could sing and dance, as well as blink!

Years later, I learned the director of that play was a young man named Luke Yankee. Luke is the son of actress Eileen Heckart (*Bus Stop, Butterflies Are Free, The 5 Mrs. Buchanans, Alice*) and we became good friends for awhile.

Here's another strange coincidence. I basically moved to California because of *Bewitched*, which starred Elizabeth Montgomery, I later lived with SueAne Langdon and her husband (after Kasey passed), and today I am friends with Eileen Heckart's son, Luke Yankee. Oddly enough, Elizabeth, SueAne, and Eileen all starred together in

A genii? "At least it's an allied line"

a (really dreadful) film called *The Victim*. (I say really dreadful as that's how SueAne describes it herself... One reason being, there isn't any ending!)

That December, Kasey was diagnosed with cancer and began the first of many surgeries. She also began radiation therapy but being

Louise and Tabatha together again. In a perfect world Tabatha would have grown up to marry Jonathan Tate.

the incredible trouper that she was, still attended her 70th birthday party at her daughter Monika's house that same year as if nothing at all was wrong!

By December 19th, Kasey, Bernard and I were off to Chicago and the set of *The Jerry Springer Show*! There we met up with Erin Murphy (Tabatha) and David and Greg Mandel (Lawrence), the twins that had originally played Adam.

Also on the stage with us were Lani O'Grady (*Eight Is Enough*), and Brandon Cruz (*The Courtship of Eddie's Father*). Today Brandon Cruz sports a rather punk look and is an exceptionally nice guy.

I don't remember a lot about the show, but I do remember an audience member calling me "The *Bewitched* Stalker"! HA! I rather liked that!

At one point, Kasey, Bernard and I were walking through the bitterly cold streets of Chicago one night and a homeless man on the street recognized Bernard as "Dr. Bombay." When the guy asked the good Dr. for money, Bernard pointed to me and said, "Talk to my manager!"

If you don't remember this particular episode of *The Jerry Springer Show*, it's because it never aired. Why? It's my understanding that the twins who played Adam refused to sign the release forms as they were the *only* ones not compensated for their appearance, because they weren't guild members.

Chapter 18
CALLING DR. BOMBAY! EMERGENCY! COME RIGHT AWAY!

I first met Bernard Fox in 1992 when we were invited to an autograph show at The Water Gardens in Santa Monica. Kasey and I had contacted him and then went to pick him up in her navy blue Jag. She made me go to the door alone. I was so nervous walking up to his front door, but Bernard was great from the onset, and we have become lifelong friends. Both of our families have been through quite a lot together and today, Bernard, his lovely wife Jacque, their daughter Amanda, and Lisa, are my second family.

In fact, tradition states that nearly every Halloween, Amanda and I create a cemetery in their front yard and I sit high in a tree by the front door and scare the hell out of unsuspecting trick-or-treaters! Of course, adding to the fear factor is Amanda, dressed as a creeped-out zombie sitting on her Harley. Lisa busies herself handing out candy and preparing an incredible dinner for us to enjoy when the fun of tricks and treats is over!

In 1995, Bernard, Sandra Gould, Kasey and I went to what was then the Warner Bros. Ranch where the original façade of the Stephen's home used in *Bewitched* still stands. I know! I know! The hair!

With Tim Allen the day *Home Improvement* blew up the house!

Chapter 18: Calling Dr. Bombay! Emergency! Come Right Away! | 105

In 1995 Mrs. Kravitz had her last *snoop* into the front window of the Stephens' home.

At the time of the above photo, the Bewitched house facade was no more than two sides of a building (left and front facing) propped up by heavy beams and supports. Thru the years it had undergone many changes from its original inception and only half of the front wall brick was still in place. But overall it is still recognizable.

In 1995, Tim Allen and the cast and crew of *Home Improvement* were going to blow it up for an episode of that show, and no one was certain if the façade would survive. Luckily, we were able to be there and document the "historic" moment with a video camera.

I have some incredible footage that was edited into a half hour DVD of Kasey, Sandra, and Bernard being interviewed on the back lot. Some of the tidbits include Sandra "whisper-yelling" "Abner!" (because the *Home Improvement* crew were filming across the street) from the front door of the exterior used for the Kravitz (and later, The Partridge Family) house.

Me interviewing Bernard by the *Fergus the Frog* (OK, OK, *Friends*) Fountain!

Some other footage I captured that day also includes our good Dr. reciting the following incantation:

"As Faierie Queen I must away,
Where mortals are, I cannot stay!"

And with his trademark Bombay gesture and the aid of some old-fashioned FX, he pops right out of the scene!

Speaking of "Dr. Bombay," Bernard fashioned his character based on a man he knew in the navy during World War II. His signature "pop out" gesture was his own invention.

Bernard also holds an interesting position in motion picture history. He's the only actor to play a survivor of the infamous *Titanic* in not one, but *two* film adaptations! In 1958's *A Night to Remember*, he played the character of "Lookout Fleet." Fleet was an employee of the Cunard Line and was in the crow's nest that fateful night. It was he who first spotted the enormous iceberg! It was also he who rang the bell and quickly alerted the captain. Fleet survived the sinking, but later became depressed over lack of work and being one of many, who were branded "bad luck." Sadly, he hanged himself in his brother-in-law's back yard sometime later.

Five years later, in 2000, a year after Sandra had passed away, we went back to the Ranch with Alice Ghostley and added more video footage to the collection.

In James Cameron's 1997 epic *Titanic*, Bernard again appeared on the big screen this time as "Col. Archibald Gracie," a man who actually went down with the ship only to resurface moments later. He was plucked out of the icy water and climbed aboard an overturned lifeboat. The all-male survivors spent the next several harrowing hours standing together in a huddle on the back of the boat while Second Officer Lightoller kept it in balance.

Once onboard the rescue ship *Carpathia*, Gracie went about collecting every survivor's story and immediately set it to paper. His was the first book ever published recounting the horrific night of April 15th 1912.

Col. Gracie would succumb to illness that he incurred from exposure after many hours in the wet and icy sea and never see his book hit print.

It's GREAT to watch "Esmeralda" pathetically utter her infamous, "Oh dear!" while standing on the front doorstep of the Stephens' home.

In 2006, only one month before Kasey suffered her fatal stroke, Valerie Fox, Bernard and Jacque's youngest daughter, passed away quite suddenly. Bernard and Jacque are like second parents to me and it was an incredibly devastating time, but one that has brought us closer together.

Ahhh, the nights I spent at Amanda's drinking, enjoying the hot tub, and sampling Lisa's incredible cooking.

CHAPTER 18: CALLING DR. BOMBAY! EMERGENCY! COME RIGHT AWAY!

Bernard "zaps" the spot in the Stephen's front yard where Samantha's weeping willow once stood.

And then there was the time that Kasey and I were at a party thrown by Amanda and Lisa. It was June and we were having an incredible time enjoying delicious food, and plenty of cosmopolitans! Kasey, being caught up in the "gaiety" of it all, suddenly leaned over and nibbled Amanda's ear. That was the first time I had ever seen Amanda speechless! It was all in good fun and Kasey later called them to say, "It looks like I *out-ed* myself at your party yesterday!" Amanda and I still get a kick out of that story!

An early 70's photo of Kasey and Dick Sargent at an unknown function. I still have that leather purse she has on the table.

Chapter 19

An Adventure in Ventura

During that same year, Kasey opted to have more neck surgery to remove a string of lymph nodes that could possibly cause more trouble down the road. Days after the surgery we found ourselves on the road to Ventura, a little beach town to the north. We used to go there a lot, as it was only forty-five minutes up the road, but felt worlds away from where we lived in the Valley. In summer, Ventura could be a good twenty degrees cooler than the Valley!

At the time, Kasey was sporting what we called her "Bride of Frankenstein" gash that ran all the way up her neck to her ear and back down under her chin! And all held together with staples! She covered it with a scarf!

Oddly enough, we happened to park the car just outside a small tattoo and piercing parlor. Immediately I could see the wheels turning in Kasey's head.

True to form, she walked in, whipped off the scarf and asked, "Could you guys do this on the other side for me?"

Everyone just stopped and stared, but Kasey loved it.

Shot on June 8, 1967 by the famed Hollywood photographer George Hurrell, this picture shows L-R Montgomery, York, Asher, White unknown crew member and episode co-star Renzo Cesana on the 1164 living room set. Of note is the hinged wall allowing us a glimpse into the soundstage.

Chapter 20
RECIPE FOR A COOKBOOK

Dawn Wells, forever immortalized as "Mary Ann," the sweetest Kansas farm girl you'd ever want to be marooned on an island with, began the trend. She penned *Mary Ann's Gilligan's Island Cookbook* with what seemed to include a *hundred* recipes for coconut cream pie alone! So Kasey and I began thinking, "Why not create a *Bewitched* cookbook in honor of Samantha Stephens?"

After all, Samantha had to learn to cook by mortal methods and many of the episodes revolved around her saving the day for McMann & Tate by preparing a magnificent meal, looking gorgeous, wooing the client, AND doing it all sans magic... well almost! Only Elizabeth Montgomery could've pulled that off with such *realism*.

Speaking of realism, Montgomery did a great job in *Bewitched* that went mostly unrecognized by the Academies. Have you ever tried to recite a rhyming incantation while at the same time trying not to sound like a complete doofus? Imagine walking up to some animal and demurely asking: "Sweetheart, is that you?" while trying to sound *normal*?

After a bit of discussion, we decided to go for it. We worked for weeks and weeks on the *Bewitched Cookbook: Magic in the Kitchen*, and could not have made it through without the incredible help of our dear friend and all around *Bewitched*-know-it-all, Steven Colbert. The three of us sat in front of the TV and watched episode after episode of *Bewitched* to get as many food references as possible.

Kasey poses with the cookbook

Off to the TV Land Network Kick-Off Party! Adding to the fun we found Bernard standing in the parking lot wearing his full-dress kilts!

Luckily, we were able to land a publisher, but sadly, some of our favorite chapters were omitted; particularly those with the "Guest Stars" and "the Clients." These included actual recipes and memories from cast members still living at the time. To this day, it irritates me that the back cover still mentions these things but they are nowhere to be found inside the book!

On April 29th of that same year, the remaining cast members of *Bewitched* were invited to the *TV Land* "Kick-Off" Party at Paramount Studios, Kasey's old stomping grounds.

We met up with Bernard and Jacque Fox in a parking lot in Studio City so we could all ride together.

Every classic TV star that was still with us at the time seemed to be there that night; the girls from *Petticoat Junction*, the guys from

My Three Sons, as well as surviving cast members of *Hazel, The Donna Reed Show*, and *The Dick Van Dyke Show*. I was surrounded by those familiar TV faces: Rob Petrie, Sally Rogers, Buddy Sorrell, Weezy Jefferson, Doc, Captain Stubing, Mr. Whipple, and even Mrs. Butterworth! The list was endless. It was truly an incredible evening!

Shortly after that night we lost Morey Amsterdam. Kasey and I attended his funeral. Now, one might think this would have been a solemn affair, but on the contrary, it was one of the funniest things I've ever witnessed! Listening to speakers like Milton Berle, Dick Van Dyke, Rose Marie, Jack Carter, Steve Allen, and Carl Reiner, with each one topping the other, I don't think the walls of that synagogue had ever contained that much laughter!

Unfortunately, one very sour memory does stay in my mind from that day—meeting Mary Tyler Moore. She certainly didn't turn *my* world on with her smile because she didn't seem to have one! Let's just say she is NOT at all the "Laura Petrie" or "Mary Richards" you might think. Rather, her role in *Ordinary People* comes to mind. Enough said.

1996 also brought some entertaining Christmas memories! Kasey's son-in-law at the time had crafted some foam angel wings for a project he was working on, so I borrowed a pair to wear to Atlanta... much to the feigned embarrassment of Kasey and my friend Darlene Wheatly. Those were the days when you could do funny things like that in an airport. Whenever people passed me they'd ask, "Are you the co-pilot?" And I'd reply, "Oh no, God is my co-pilot!" or "I'm just on my way home to sit on top of the Christmas tree... it may hurt but someone's got to do it!"

I stashed the wings in the overhead compartment for the flight and put them on when I landed in Atlanta. As expected, Mom and Dad were there waiting to pick me up and were talking with a lady they had just met when I came thru in my wings. They pretended they didn't know me. So, of course, I ran to them yelling, "HI MOM! HI DAD!" Truth be told, they actually loved it! Besides, they're used to me by now, if that's possible...

In line to board my flight. Sure couldn't do this today!

The many faces of Elizabeth Montgomery from the episode Weep No More My Willow photographed on August 6, 1968 by Art Saye. Kasey would often recall that "after a scene was finished Bill would keep the camera running and NOT say 'Cut!' just to make Elizabeth keep reacting to what just happened... it bordered on cruelty at times" laughed Kasey, "but Elizabeth never stopped until Bill said to. Then she would shoot him a dirty look. But Bill always got what he wanted from her performance and it shows in every episode."

Chapter 21
AGNES OF GOD

Kasey always described her in one word..."GRAND"... She was *exactly* what you expected.

Agnes always threw the very first Christmas party of the season in Hollywood. Usually it was around her birthday, December 6th, and Kasey was invited several times. Agnes Moorehead's Christmas parties were *legendary* in Hollywood circles and it was *the* place to be.

Kasey remembered being impressed by how the wine at dinner was served. "Sitting next to everyone's place setting was one of those glass grape clusters that expensive wines used to come in. You would just refill your own glass from your own private reserve! It was quite elegant." She also remembered Debbie Reynolds attending one of the parties and how much Agnes just raved about her.

Bernard Fox's recollections of Agnes included the time he worked for her. "Agnes would teach acting at her home to a small group of gay men, many of whom lived with her from time to time and did odd jobs around the house. Mostly her teaching skills consisted of pontificating about her own illustrious career! Those same students were EXPECTED at her home every Sunday, where she would hold church services."

Speaking of which, when I first got to Los Angeles Kasey and I would go to Hollywood quite often. It always was a bit "seedy," but is looking better today, with the advent of the new Kodak Theatre (now the Dolby).

It's hard to believe that Agnes initially didn't want to do *Bewitched* and was pretty appalled when the pilot sold. But all *Bewitched* fans can breathe a sigh of relief and thank the *real* God that she did!

At the corner of Hollywood and Vine there used to be a parking lot, and on the wall surrounding it, someone had spray painted "Agnes Moorehead is GOD!" It had been there since the late sixties, and every time they would try and paint over it, someone would come right along and put it back! The last time her name was spelled "Mooreheab," but everyone still got the message.

Kasey also told me that Agnes never truly accepted the change in Darrin's. She was overheard to have once said in regard to the new look of the show, "I *dislike* change."

In 1995, when Kasey and I were doing research for the *Bewitched Cookbook: Magic in the Kitchen*, we were lucky enough to visit Columbia Studios, which had recently taken over the old M-G-M lot.

While there, we were allowed to wander around by ourselves. During our exploration we happened upon the largest soundstage built during M-G-M's heyday—Stage 26. This was the very soundstage where Judy Garland first put sequined slipper to painted yellow spiral to begin her journey down the yellow-brick road to find the Wizard of Oz. (Talk about hallowed ground!) I will say, the mind-numbing effect that one is actually standing there is inconceivable!

February 23, 1996 Sony's Wardrobe Dept. (and once M-G-M's). Can you imagine the costumes once made here? We're talking Ruby Slippers!

Later, we were shown around the wardrobe department. Being the two curious souls that we were, we asked if we could see what they had kept of Agnes'.

After looking through some dresses and boxes with her name on them, Kasey and I stumbled upon an *incredible* find! We had uncovered Agnes Moorehead's last season "Endora" costume from *Bewitched*—the last "flying suit" she ever wore! The studio didn't even realize they had it, because it was not listed *anywhere* in their inventory!

Agnes in her on-set *Bewitched* dressing room holding the Emmy she won for *The Wild Wild West*.

As we peeked inside one of the last remaining boxes, THERE IT WAS… a neatly folded lavender chiffon gown, with an underskirt of fuchsia (which made it look darker in color and brighter than the earlier versions) tucked away, and hidden beneath some tissue paper; probably having been there since the last episode of *Bewitched* was filmed.

I was allowed the privilege of placing it on a mannequin and I took advantage of this rare opportunity by snapping tons of photos! Sony Pictures was glad we unearthed it as well. Since our "find," they have made sure that Endora's last flying suit is no longer quietly tucked away somewhere, but on display at various events.

For those die-hard costumers and seamstresses that are reading this, I know your next question: "How was it made?" The way the gown is fashioned is a bit deceiving and not exactly made as one might think. The purple collar isn't actually part of the cape. It *is* in fact a part of the dress. The collar is split up the back and held together with hooks and eyes. I suppose they had their reasons for designing it that way, (but with my background in costume design, it would have been easier if it were part of the cape!).

Though these stories may shed some unknown details about our beloved "Endora," another way to find out more about Agnes Moorehead is to read the book by Charles Tranberg, "*I Love the Illusion.*"

And giving credit where credit is due, I'd like to let you know that the title of his book came from Kasey herself during an interview with Charles. Once, while working on *Bewitched*, Kasey approached Agnes and asked her favorite thing about acting. Her response? "I love the illusion!"

Chapter 22
THE IDES OF MARCH

In the spring of 1997, Kasey found a small lump in her breast. Wasting no time, we headed straight back to UCLA where Kasey had earlier gone through all the surgeries and radiation for her throat cancer. The biopsy was found to be cancerous.

I remember Kasey coming out to the waiting room where I was sitting and giving me the bad news. She wondered what she should do. We talked about the options she had discussed with the doctors with removal seeming to be the best option. I remember telling her that at 72 years of age, there was a lot left to do in life and that she should have it removed.

She took that advice but spent the next year trying different cosmetic procedures that always made her uncomfortable and unhappy. She later regretted those post-surgeries.

Kasey had many different surgeries while I was with her: cancer surgeries, knee surgery, breast surgeries, and "female" surgeries. Fortunately, they never seemed to affect her for very long. She was blessed with an incredible stamina and healing ability.

Kasey spent most of that December in the hospital, which left very little time to think about—much less get anything ready for the holidays. But after finding out she would be coming home in a day or two, I decided at the last minute to go find a Christmas tree for our condo.

It was a rainy, dreary December evening, but I found a HUGE Christmas tree at a great price. Our living room ceiling ranged in height from ten to sixteen feet, and this beauty was probably eleven feet tall! So I bought it, tied it to the roof of the car, got it home, and dragged that heavy, wet, dead-weight evergreen up the *thirty-six* steps to our condo. After I managed to get it over the railing (because it wouldn't make the turn through the gate), I set it up, and strung what seemed like *hundreds* of lights. By the time I had finished, I was exhausted.

I made a quick call to Domino's and then phoned Sandy Gould to tell her about my Christmas surprise for Kasey. She loved the idea and also gave me a piece of important advice—"Don't plug in the lights until that wet tree has dried out!" HA!

After a short break, I got right back to work because I wanted to get the tree finished and the rest of the house decorated that night, because Kasey would be coming home the following evening.

That next night, I picked Kasey up at the hospital and drove straight to the condo. I could hardly wait to see the look on her face, and I'll never forget her reaction when she walked through the front door. Not suspecting a thing, her mouth dropped open as she raised her eyes from floor to ceiling. "Welcome home!" I said. Immediately, she began to puddle up. We toasted each other with a glass of holiday cheer and just sat for the longest time, admiring our beautiful tree and eating apples, cheese and crackers!

Cancer touched my life twice that year. I was briefly acquainted with actress Gail Davis, who was best known for her 1950s TV role of "Annie Oakley." She and her daughter came into the store where I was working and I helped them choose some fabric for her draperies. Later, I went to her small apartment and installed the cornice boxes that she herself had made.

Gail, who was undergoing chemotherapy for cancer, had lost all of her hair. Fittingly, she wore a western bandana.

She and Kasey tried to sell a fantastic Western-themed script that Kasey had written called *The Great Republic of Rough & Ready!*

Rough & Ready is a small town in Northern California that actually seceded from the union in 1850, becoming the world's smallest nation within a nation! It's an amazing story that is rarely taught in schools and has not yet been touched by Hollywood! After all, the entire Civil War was fought to keep the South from succeeding, so how did this little tiny, gold rich town manage it years before?

We eventually stopped hearing anything from Gail and later found out that she had suddenly passed away from cancer on March 15, 1997.

Chapter 23
ALICE DOESN'T LIVE HERE ANYMORE...

Alice age 11!

My first encounter with Alice Ghostley happened in 1991, while I was still living in Georgia. Feeling empowered by my original, successful phone call to Kasey, I decided to try shouting out a "Yoo-Hoo" to Esmeralda. At the time, she was currently starring as the daffy but loveable Bernice Clifton on *Designing Women*.

After reaching Alice on the phone, I described my project and asked if she'd like to be a part of *Bewitched... Again!*

Very sweetly she declined, saying that she was under contract to her current show, and wouldn't be able to participate. Extremely disappointed, I thought, "Oh well, that's that," having no idea that she would later become a part of my life.

Several years later, our paths would cross again when Kasey and I called her to participate in our *Bewitched* cookbook. Alice admitted that she didn't cook, but her husband, Felice (Orlandi) did. *Designing Women* had ended by that time, and while Bernice Clifton was fondly remembered, Esmeralda was *revered* by countless fans all over the world! Fortunately, Alice understood this and was more than happy to participate.

After we had chatted more about the cookbook and it was time to hang up, she said to me, "Thank you, "Flower!" I have never before, nor since been referred to as "Flower," but if Esmeralda wanted to call me "Flower" it was OK with me!!!

Through the years Kasey and I kept in contact with Alice and visited her at her home many times, once to even interview her on camera. Recently, I watched it again and noticed that I was so excited I couldn't stop talking the whole time! But even with my mouth going ninety-to-nothing, I treasure that video interview with Alice.

After Kasey became sick for the fourth and final time, she and Alice would occasionally chat as Alice was having health issues too. We still hoped against hope that Sony would wake up and consider green-lighting *Bewitched... Again!* (talk about the project that wouldn't die). Having rewritten it countless times, the final revision had Esmeralda playing her role from a seated position, since Alice could no longer walk without assistance due to a previous stroke. "It's easier for her to just fade out sitting on a sofa arm and fade back in sitting on a desk chair," Kasey would say. It helped keep them going.

We had even worked the script around Kasey's inability to speak clearly, due to the tracheal tube in her throat.

How would this be accomplished? We researched her dialogue from past *Bewitched* episodes and any time Louise Tate needed to speak, her voice would be culled from old episodes and Kasey would then lip sync to herself. You can't imagine what we went through to

Chapter 23: Alice Doesn't Live Here Anymore

The final resting place of Alice and Felice.

try and make this happen. But sadly, Sony never realized its potential and still doesn't.

My chapter title is a bit misleading. Although Alice has since passed away, she will forever be at her home on Reklaw Avenue in Studio City. She was cremated, and her ashes laid to rest next to her husband Felice, under the large orange tree in their backyard.

I was grateful to be given Alice's guest room furniture and many other odds and ends from her home after she passed on. As I was leaving with my truck laden with mementos and treasures from "Esmeralda," I noticed a broom standing all by itself by the kitchen door.

DOROTHY (to the witch's guard): *The broom. May we have it?*

GUARD: *Please. And take it with you.*

That was the beginning of my broom collection. I now have several that are signed by Hollywood's best, including one from Billie "Witchiepoo" Hayes.

Me, Alice and Felice

Chapter 24

KASEY'S COMMERCIAL

1998 was a year filled with ups and downs.

My father passed away on August 3rd. In early October Kasey's former husband, Bud Lewis, died.

Kasey had landed her first commercial audition in years and was set to shoot the day he passed away. She came to my room and told me, and I remember her not wanting to cry so she'd look alright for the commercial shoot. Now, some may find this crass but remember they had not been together for nearly 25 years, and while terribly saddened by it all she decided "The show must go on!"

Kasey was very proud of getting cast in that commercial. At the age of seventy-three, she looked young enough to be playing the wife of a forty-eight year old man! She never revealed her true age to the producers, and didn't tell them that her ex-husband had died that day until the shoot was over. What a trouper!

When the family finally decided to have Bud's memorial service, (he had been cremated) we marched up a hillside in Zuma Beach, so his ashes could be scattered in the wind. Funny thing, Bud Lewis always *hated* me and never cared much for his stepson Jay, and ironically, it fell to the two of us to cart his ass up that steep mountainside in a bag!

Bernard Fox gets "hosed down" for this scene from Weep No More My Willow shot on July, 11, 1968.

Chapter 25
America Gets a Step-Dad: The Second Darrin

What more can be said about the infamous change of Darrins on *Bewitched*? It's been the butt of jokes for forty plus years now. While writers were spending *sixteen* years writing what became the greatly disappointing and widely panned *Bewitched* movie, every writer thought he had the original idea of "switching Darrin's" half way through, because it was clever. Needless to say, fans thought that joke was old then, and still do. Still, it might have helped that film!

Sadly, the change in Darrin's was just a necessary evil. One man could no longer perform the role, and another needed to step up to the plate and do his best.

Actually, Sargent's Darrin isn't that bad. If you watch carefully in his series debut, it's Elizabeth that's bad!

Yes *Bewitched* fans, I know... I just committed the *ultimate* sacrilege. But truth be told, she was so busy compensating, that the normally perfect luminary was adding nothing but a bit of frantic acting.

By Dick's second season, things seem to be on more of an upswing, but by his third and final season of the series, Elizabeth is all but *phoning* in her part! She was so ready for the show and that part of her life to be over that she couldn't get away fast enough! And poor Dick Sargent always gets the blame.

However, the Sargent years did leave us with some great episodes—especially the ones shot in Salem.

Bewitched was the first sitcom to ever go on location to film, therefore making TV history. And Salem should thank its lucky stars. Those episodes of *Bewitched* put Salem on the map as a popular tourist destination. Roughly a million tourists fill Salem (mostly in October) annually. A town once known for trying to sweep its witch-hysteria under the cauldron, Salem has finally embraced it because of the money it brings in. Before the witches came back to town Salem didn't even have a museum dedicated to that unfortunate event centuries ago. So...

...when TV Land decided to pay homage to the show by erecting a statue of "Samantha," they chose Salem, Massachusetts instead of Westport, Connecticut—a decision not without controversy.

On the flip side, it helped clean up a derelict park, home to transients, and reopened long shuttered businesses. Today, the Lappin Park area is a bustling, thriving tourist destination. (Thanks, Sam!)

Dick Sargent, who will probably always be known as "the second Darrin," was a *very* nice man. I got to know him during my first two years in LA; the last two years of his life. He was charming and fun—an absolute sweetheart. His original surname was Cox. He used to delight in telling people that his mother never quite understood why he decided to change his name from "Dick Cox" to Dick Sargent.

Chapter 25: America Gets a Step-Dad: The Second Darrin

The *living* cast, the *bronze* cast and me! The coldest June day in Salem, MA 2005.

During my first March in L.A., Kasey and I called him for a little get-together we were hosting at her acting studio. This soirée included Sandy Gould, Erin Murphy, Kasey, Dick, and me. It was like old home week for everyone from the cast, and I was beside myself as you can well imagine. These people had not seen each other in twenty years, and here they were getting reacquainted because they wanted to do *my* project, *Bewitched... Again!* Surreal is the only way to describe how it felt to be sitting right in the middle of it all!

Everyone was so pleased to see each other again, and kept saying, "Why haven't we done this before?" I remember Dick kept saying, "I didn't think any of you liked me!" He couldn't have been more wrong.

Another adventure we all shared was the time that Kasey, Sandy, and I made plans to meet Dick at a gay nightclub in West Hollywood called Rage. There I was, sitting amidst these *Bewitched* icons, watching all these guys do double-takes as they walked by. For those that were bold enough to ask who I was, Dick introduced me as his son, "Adam"!

> **DICK SARGENT**
>
> 5/11/92
>
> Mark Wood
> c/o Hollywood Underground Network
> Suite # 1
> North Hollywood, CA 91601
>
> Dear Mark,
>
> A brief note to tell you that I think you're an extremely talented young man, that your ideas for "Bewitched Again" are great, and that I would love to be a part of the project.
>
> This is one tough town, but your devotion to your plans are admirable, and I hope you can breech the walls. I think you should and that you can.
>
> All the best to you,
>
> *Dick Sargent*

To all of America, he may just be Darrin #2, but to me, he'll always be my favorite *step-dad!*

I talked to Dick one last time in June of 1994. All of us were genuinely heartsick when he told us that his prostate cancer had returned. Like so many others from *Bewitched*, it was far too soon, and Dick was far too young.

His memorial service was held on July 24th, 1994 at Forest Lawn Cemetery Burbank in the Old North Church (a replica of the church made famous by Paul Revere). Seated on the pew with Kasey and myself were Bernard Fox, his wife Jacque, Erin Murphy, Alice Ghostley, and Sandra Gould.

Shortly before the service began, the doors in the back of the church quietly opened, and in walked Elizabeth Montgomery. She knew that arriving early would have caused the press to focus on her, diminishing the reason we were all there.

Though I tried not to stare, I couldn't help but notice that Elizabeth looked absolutely radiant! Her hair was long again, not curly, as it was in the Edna Buchanan TV movies, but with a more relaxed flip, reminiscent of Samantha Stephens. She wore a burgundy dress and heels that accentuated her shapely legs, and she looked phenomenal!

No one would have believed that she too, would be gone only eight months later.

After the service, we were all invited over to Dick's house; a lovely cottage built into the mountains of the Hollywood Hills that overlooked the valley. It was especially beautiful that night, watching fireworks shoot into the sky from Universal Studios.

As we walked inside, I found it a little odd that the kitchen was in the process of being remodeled. The refrigerator and stove had been moved and were sitting at odd angles, and all the flooring had been torn out, exposing the sub-floor.

On an easel in the living room was a large, color, abstract painting of Dick. But noticeably absent from the rest of the house were mementoes of his career; the exception was a color photo of him and Elizabeth used as a *TV Guide* cover shortly after he took over the role of Darrin Stephens.

This was also the evening that Sandra Gould introduced me to Elizabeth Montgomery. Now I finally had the opportunity to tell her how much *Bewitched* meant to me, but I had also been forewarned that I had to tread lightly, as this was *not* her favorite subject.

According to Kasey and many others, Elizabeth could never bring herself to enjoy the accolades of playing Samantha Stephens. She suffered inner conflict and emotional turmoil over the very thing that brought so much joy to millions of people the world over.

I was able to talk with her for a little while, so knowing her feelings about *Bewitched*, I prefaced the conversation with, "I'm the guy you probably never wanted to meet... But I have to tell you how much I love and adore you, and everything you ever did, because *Bewitched* literally changed my life!" She was actually attentive so I proceeded to tell her how. I explained the *Bewitched... Again!* premise and she actually said that she liked it (then again, what else would she say to a fan... in public... at a funeral... of "Darrin"...?)

She had been very sweet and very cordial, but also politely trying to get away from the conversation. I don't think she really knew what to say, and wanted to avoid talking about *Bewitched*. She explained that she had "moved on" from that part of her career, but was quick to acknowledge that no matter what she did... And that was when I politely interjected, "Even if you shot the President".... And she laughed and said, "Exactly! Whatever is written about me will probably say, "Former *Bewitched* Star Shoots President..." and that was more or less, the extent of our conversation. No, I did NOT ask her to twitch her nose and no, it was not the time or place to ask for a photo.

But despite her misgivings, Elizabeth Montgomery was an incredibly warm and wonderful human being whose time on Earth was cut way too short.

The following evening, Kasey and I decided to break out the Ouija board, which we had done quite often before. I know what you're thinking, but it was so much fun and led to quite an experience.

After only a few moments of playing around with the board, we were both certain that we had Dick "coming through loud and clear," and he sounded very *angry*! (Work with me here...) He seemed to be annoyed with Albert, his partner at the time.

To make a long story short, Dick seemed bothered about something that he had put on a piece of film and had apparently hidden in the shower head in the upstairs bathroom!

Our *mission* (should we decide to accept it) was to retrieve it, and give it to Elizabeth Montgomery, who would know exactly what to do with it! Okay, I know it sounds a bit far-fetched, but I *swear* to you, that was the message that came through that night on the Ouija board! We recorded it on a cassette so anytime you can come and hear it! LOL. With that, Kasey and I found ourselves off on yet another adventure!

Enlisting the aid of Sandy Gould, we managed to get Albert to invite us over to dinner. Oh yes…!

As luck would have it, the small downstairs guest bath was also being remodeled and out of commission, which coincided perfectly with our plan.

Kasey came prepared with a pair of needle nose pliers hidden in her purse. Sandra had a wrench! Sometime during the course of dinner, she quietly slipped them to me, and I politely excused myself to go to the restroom. Just as we hoped, I was directed *upstairs*!

Kasey and Sandy kept everyone busy as I unexpectedly encountered *two* upstairs bathrooms; a master and a guest.

I chose the guest bath first, where the shower head unscrewed easily.

But much to my disappointment I found *NOTHING*!!

Knowing that time was fleeting, I quickly rushed into the master bath, pliers in hand, to find that this shower head would not budge an inch, no matter how hard I tried!

Also knowing that one can only go to the bathroom for so long before people begin to worry, I had no choice but to go back downstairs and tell the gals what had happened when no one else was listening. Needless to say, we were very disappointed. And Sandy, who didn't want to give up, kept wanting to go back and try it all over again!

Often we couldn't help but wonder, "Was it really there?!" But because of limited time and a stubborn showerhead, I guess we'll never know.

All was not lost though. We did receive a great parting gift that evening, which I found out about when we got back home. "Klepto-Kasey" had *lifted* a small black and white picture she found on the floor partially hidden under the rug in the dining room. It was a photo of Dick when he was a 13-year-old cadet in military school!

One last bit about Dick (as I sit here editing this four years after I first wrote it). I just came across a small tin wind up cat that he had given me. Sargent used to collect vintage and antique tin wind-up toys.

Darrin Stephens, 13 year-old cadet.

Chapter 26
Farewell to the 1990s

1999 saw an increased activity in our writing. With all the holiday parties we had hosted, and the decorations we'd carefully hand-made, Kasey and I decided to give Martha Stewart a run for her money! We found a publisher willing to take a chance on Kasey's name, and together, created our first craft book, *Halloween Crafts: Eerily, Elegant Décor*.

Trying to find a location to shoot the pictures to be included in the book wasn't an easy task. Feeling strongly that Hallowe'en should always have an antique or Victorian look, we were somewhat disappointed having just been turned down by a chain called The Spaghetti Factory, which showcased a lot of really impressive antiques. But luckily I then remembered having driven by a museum called The Stagecoach Inn in Newbury Park, about eighteen miles up the road from us.

We met with the director, Sandy Hildebrandt, and she was happy to accommodate our request.

This particular location couldn't have been more perfect—a rustic, Victorian looking hotel with a barn, pioneer cabin, parlor, and a haunted cradle. It was just right!

We shot pictures in every nook and cranny we could find, and ended up using the same location for our next three books.

(Trying to make the pioneer cabin look like Christmas with artificial snow in 100-degree heat was an incredible challenge, but not impossible.) Some shots called for us to put on turtle necks and coats in order to make the picture look like the dead of winter. Because of the stifling heat, we were pretty miserable, but laughed about it later and were very pleased with the final result.

As repayment, Kasey and I decorated the museum for every major holiday over the next two years. Later, we got involved with the museum's annual October program called "An Evening on The Conejo" (Conejo means rabbit and is the name of the valley in which the Stagecoach Inn sits).

During the event, guides would take visitors on a walking tour through the park trails, while encountering actors playing people from a century past. They would eventually take us into the barn, the cabin, and finally the hotel itself. Everyone being dressed in full period costumes of the era and the festivities taking place at night by lantern light added greatly to an entertaining and pleasurable evening—one with an extremely authentic feeling.

Kasey and I were in the first scene the guests saw on their journey. Kasey played "Momma" and I played "Professor Montenari," the Medicine Man.

The scene would open as Kasey is heard complaining how I brought her out to this "Godforsaken" land. I'd turn a deaf ear and continue to hawk my snake oil to the audience!

I must have been pretty convincing because on more than one occasion, there were some guests who actually wanted to purchase my doctored-up beer bottles for a buck each! Not wanting to step out of character, what else could I do but gladly accept their money?!

"…with this elixir, you will soar as the falcon soars, run with the speed of gazelles and command the powers of Earth and Sky! It is the same magic, authentic potion used by the priests of Isis and Osiris in the days of the pharaohs of Egypt. When Cleopatra first plied her womanly wiles on the likes of Marc Antony and Julius Caesar and… uhm… uh…'Boston Blackie'!"

It was left up to us to come up with our own lines. If you recognized any of the above it is because we plagiarized everything from Professor Marvel's lines to Dorothy in *The Wizard of Oz*, to the opening sequence used in the Saturday morning kids program, *The Secrets of Isis*! And Kasey would flirt unmercifully with any "gentleman caller" that came down the trail! Even offer her "room key" at the hotel! Brazen!

You might find this hard to believe, but we were a hit! HA!

We would do the show six times an evening for two consecutive weekends. Then, being the first scene to finish, we'd make our way

KR as "Momma"

to the makeshift dining room in the basement and eat a free dinner that those in the audience had to pay for. Show business does have its perks! We stayed in character and "entertained the troops" half the night!

While out driving one day I was lamenting to Kasey, "Where are we ever going to find such a tree?"

In what was split-second perfect timing, she replied, "How about there?!" as she pointed to the most perfectly gnarled, dead tree that was sitting right in someone's front yard.

Oh how I coveted that tree from the minute I saw it.

Then, miracle of miracles! One day those very homeowners were having a yard sale! So we stopped the car and told them that we didn't really come to buy anything at the yard sale. We were more interested in buying something in their *yard*, as I pointed to the old, twisted tree. The owner looked a bit perplexed, but rather quickly said, "Fifteen dollars"! HA!

My friend Julia and I dug it up (it weighed a ton for something dead), put it in the back of her truck and carted it home.

As perfect as it looks in the picture above, nothing compared to seeing it in person.

On April 19, 1998, we attended the Elizabeth Montgomery Charity Auction held in Beverly Hills.

The usual cast was there—Kasey, Bernard, Sandra, Erin, me and this time, Erin's twin sister Diane. The only thing I ended up winning was a blue and white denim jacket that Elizabeth had once worn. We were all a bit disappointed that there was nothing much from *Bewitched* at the auction, but one of the highlights of the day was when Erin and some male dancers did a rendition of the *Bewitched* theme on stage, just as Elizabeth had performed it on *The Hollywood Palace* many years earlier.

Kasey and I had also gotten wind of an upcoming yard sale to be held at Elizabeth's former home on Benedict Canyon Rd. on June 13, 1998. We attended, but I could still kick myself every time I think of the fact that the green shaded two-armed lamp used in the Stephen's foyer on *Bewitched* was for sale and I didn't get it! Ugh!!

1999, as we all remember, ended with the Y2K scare.

Can you remember how up in arms we all were then? Kasey and I celebrated that New Years Eve at Amanda and Lisa's house, along

For one of the decorating ideas in our first Halloween book, I wanted to do a haunted tree like the one in the Ray Bradbury book, *The Halloween Tree*; something dead and gnarled and loaded with grinning Jack O'lanterns.

L to R- KR, Bernard, Me, Sandra, and Erin at the Elizabeth Montgomery Benefit Auction

with Bernard and Jacque Fox. As we watched the ball in Times Square fall, we also waited for planes to fall from the sky, and computers that run the world to blow up! We waited and waited... but nothing. We did hear some fireworks but that was the biggest bang we got out of that New Years Eve.

> FUN SIDE NOTE: Just months before her passing in 1999, I saw Ellen "Grandma Walton" Corby at the Motion Picture Hospital. She could no longer talk and was in a wheel chair. Our eyes met and I happily exclaimed, "Grandma Walton!" She got this huge smile on her face and puddled up. I gave her a big hug. It was a nice moment, and I think it made her day to be recognized and called "Grandma" one more time.

Me and some of my treasures from the Elizabeth Montgomery yard sale.

Dick York peers thru the door to the kitchen in the episode Business Italian Style shot on June, 8th, 1968.

Chapter 27

BAD BLOOD ON THE SET

OK, here we go, the moment all of you have been waiting for... "dirt." But don't get too excited, there isn't much!

To most people, *Bewitched* looked like one big happy family, but that wasn't always the case. Bill Asher was a dear friend (oddly, I am editing this chapter on the same day that I got the call from his wife Meredith and told of Bill's passing. It is 12:04 PM, West Coast time on July 16, 2012), but I am told there was a bit of an autocratic attitude with him and Elizabeth, especially after season two. Kasey and I discussed it often. She had her theories.

Bill and Elizabeth saw a chance to get ahead, and after the first two years, there was tension between Bill and then producer, Danny Arnold.

Somehow, during persuasive renegotiations of their contracts, the Ashers were able to oust Danny Arnold, and along with him went Irene Vernon (the original Louise Tate. It was reported that Irene left the show "to go into real estate." She *did* go into real estate, but would've stayed with *Bewitched* for its entire run if things had been different. Unfortunately, Arnold had brought her in, and the Ashers were cleaning house.

Also, as stated earlier, "the older man and the trophy wife" was fast becoming the "in" thing. Irene Vernon was truly funny and wonderful in the role; even Kasey agreed with that, but then there's—*ratings*.

I was also told that the Ashers even wanted to get rid of David White, because he and Danny Arnold were very good friends, but at that point, ABC stepped in and said, "Absolutely not!! David White is the show's fourth main character. He stays!" In time, things were eventually smoothed out, and they all ended up becoming good friends.

Sandra Gould had her share of problems with the Ashers as well. Back in the early 1990s, when the networks were doing all those "clip" shows that interviewed former cast members, one particular show called *TV's All-Time Favorites* (1995) wanted to do a "favorite neighbor" segment and asked permission to include "Samantha Stephens and Gladys Kravitz." They specifically wanted to use Sandra Gould's portrayal of the role because she was more widely known to the audience as Mrs. Kravitz, due to the many years of color-only re-runs. (All of Alice Pearce's episodes had been shot in black-and-white).

No matter which Gladys is your favorite, Sandra Gould *was* at the time the better known of the two. It took everyone by surprise when Elizabeth Montgomery refused to allow them to use a clip unless they used one with Alice Pearce. I asked Sandra if she knew why, and she sadly replied, "I don't think she ever really liked me *or* my Gladys Kravitz."

Although Elizabeth never acted nasty to Sandra on the set, William Asher apparently did. According to Sandra, there were many times when he would call her "Alice" instead of "Sandra." And that did not bode well with the second Mrs. K. She felt that he was doing it deliberately.

The day finally came when she'd had enough, and in front of God and everyone, began to throw a full-fledged temper tantrum right there on the set! She freely admitted to screaming and kicking things, and then running off to her dressing room, refusing to come out until Bill came in to apologize. Surprisingly, he did come to her dressing room to apologize, and according to Sandra, she also made him *kiss her foot*! She swore he actually did, and she used to laugh (and gloat) a little when telling that one!

More than once, Kasey said that she and Elizabeth had their moments as well, and during the last couple of seasons of *Bewitched*, Kasey wasn't used on the show very much. One theory that always floated around was that Elizabeth always worried when other pretty women were on the set:

Chris Noel, a lovely blonde actress in the episode "Love is Blind" (with a pre-Batman Adam West), didn't get along with Elizabeth at all. She said that Elizabeth was especially cold to her. She was of the opinion that it was due to Elizabeth's jealousy. If you'll notice "pretty" girls most only played bad clients or terrible witches. Also, episodes were becoming more costly, and if the character of Louise could be taken care of via the phone, it was, in a word—cheaper.

As both the Asher marriage and the show began to fade at the beginning of season seven, Kasey remembered that Elizabeth stopped wearing Samantha's traditional heart-shaped necklace, which had been a present from Bill at the beginning of *Bewitched*. It was later replaced by an "S" for Samantha. She also showed up in the make-up room one day wearing a button that simply stated, "New Game in Town"!

Kasey said that Elizabeth was the one who stopped season nine in its tracks. "There was supposed to be a ninth season because the Ashers had signed a three year contract to continue for seasons seven, eight, and nine. But in the end, Elizabeth eventually left the set, left her house, left her husband, and left the country with the assistant director!"

How true? I don't know. But that's what was told to me by more than just Kasey.

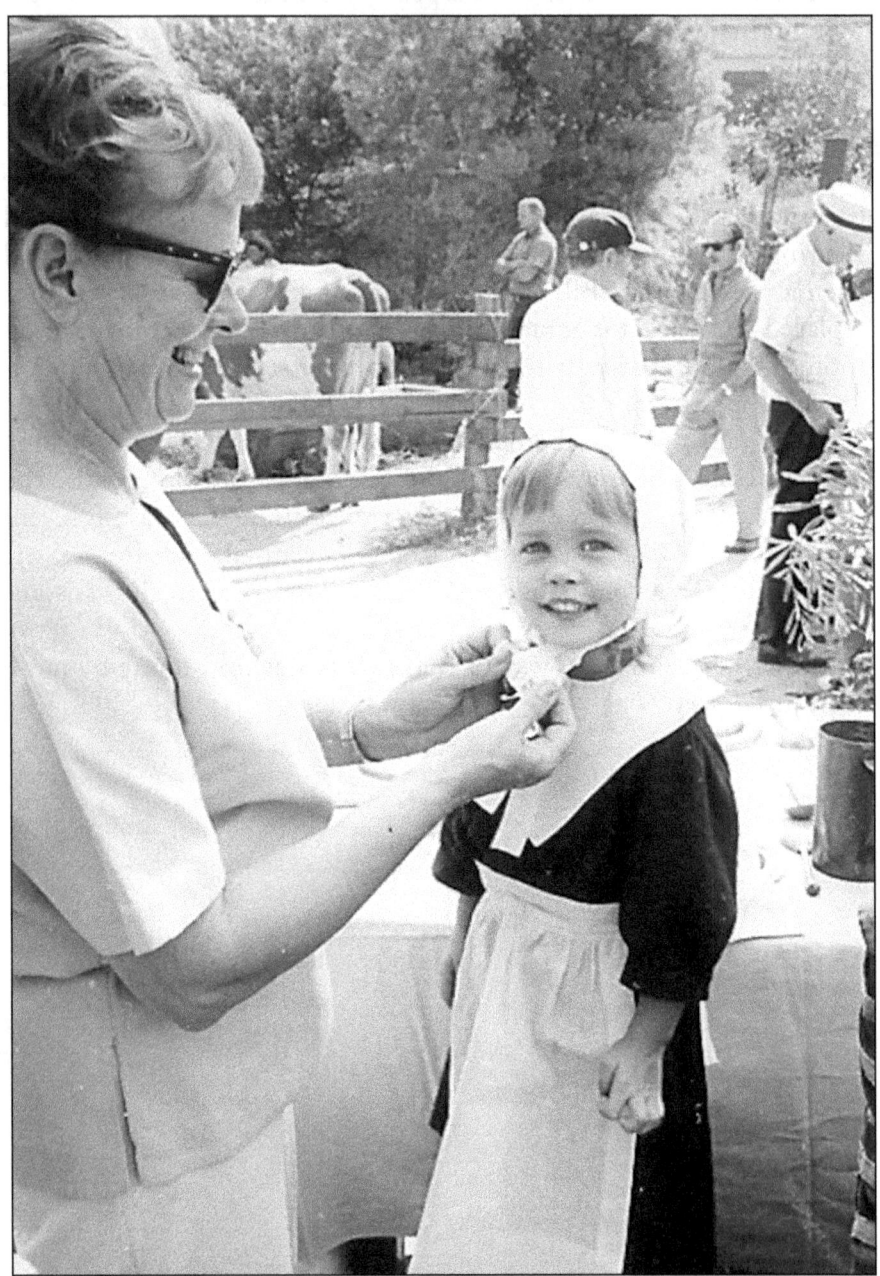

"Peanuts" the hairdresser "Pilgrim-izes" Tabatha (Erin Murphy) for Thanksgiving dinner in the episode Samantha's Thanksgiving to Remember shot on September 21st, 1967.

Chapter 28
A Bit More Bewitched...Again

During one of the many meetings we had at Sony regarding *Bewitched... Again!*, we had somehow gotten to the top executive in charge of sitcom development... *again*.

This time, we had done even more homework. Kasey and I had polled over a thousand fans via the "new" internet to gauge their interest in the project. We printed EVERY response. Two reams of paper.

We walked into the executive's office and I began my pitch.

I looked down at the glass coffee table in her office. "These are the people that would like to see our *Bewitched* reunion/new series."

WHAM!!!

I dropped the thousand responses on top of the glass table.

"These are the people that would like to see Sony's current feature film attempt." As I released them, three (yes THREE) pitiful pages fluttered from my hand.

"Point well taken," was all this executive could say.

This wonderful lady really went to bat for us, but again, it was to no avail. Even within the confines of the same company, the feature film department would NOT release the rights back to the television department. As you know, the film was eventually made, but opened to dismal ratings and reviews.

My favorite quote was from one film critic who said: "You know a film is bad when it leaves you wishing Dick *Sargent* was playing Darrin!" (Dick, wherever you are, forgive me. But it is a funny line and we all get his point!)

At least to some degree, Kasey and I were vindicated; the feature film speaks for itself. Thus, proving a new adage I continue to stand by...

...Never let a professional do a fan's job!

Shortly after our meeting at Sony, our friend Steve turned 50. Steve had us flown down to Florida where he lived at the time to celebrate. And what a celebration it was! His backyard pool had been covered with tables and chairs, and the table arrangements had more flowers in them than Munchkinland! At midnight, fireworks shot out of those flowers right over everyone's head! The biggest surprise of the evening was the entertainment. Steve had a barge that floated up the canal to his backyard and after dinner we were all treated to a concert by Patti LaBelle! What a kick listening to Patti LaBelle on a backyard barge!

I also recall a Christmas party Steve gave in 2001. This time, we had to go "cross-dressed" as our favorite movie/TV star. The entertainment that night was the well-known impressionist Jim Bailey performing as the legendary Judy Garland. Kasey was dressed as Michael Jackson (complete with sequined glove) and I was dressed as Glinda, the Good Witch of the North, in 300 yards of pink netting! Bailey took one look at me and said, "I see Billie Burke is here. Billie dear, you haven't changed in 50 years... Not even your *dress*!"

CHAPTER 28: A BIT MORE *BEWITCHED...AGAIN*

It takes nerve to put some of these photos in a book!

Aunt Clara (Marion Lorne) and Mrs. Kravitz (Sandra Gould) rest between shots on the Screen Gems/Columbia Ranch while shooting Samantha's Thanksgiving to Remember, September 21st, 1967.

Chapter 29

THE GLORIOUS GALS OF M-G-M

If Darrin Stephens were asked to write a slogan for the biggest Hollywood studio there ever was, he might have aptly chosen: "The Bigger They Are, the Harder They Fall" instead of M-G-M's traditional: "More Stars Than There Are In Heaven."

Sadly, in the early 1970s, M-G-M opted to close its doors for good, sell off its studio, build the M-G-M Grand Hotel in Las Vegas, and move to a single high rise rather than going the route of Universal Studios and selling tickets so eager fans could tour the most famous back-lot in Hollywood history.

Can you imagine what that might have been like? We could be reliving the burning of Atlanta, journeying down the yellow brick road, Meeting in St. Louis, and perhaps through the magic of technology, even dancing with Gene Kelly while singing in the rain! If the powers that be had only realized before it was too late... oh Hollywood... you will NEVER learn.

Among all the studios in their heyday, M-G-M was hands down, the most glamorous and prestigious of them all!

Much of its enduring legacy should be attributed to the immense talent of the actors and actresses who were a part of that golden era of Hollywood. I was lucky enough to know a few of those iconic stars.

VIRGINIA O'BRIEN

Virginia O'Brien was an actress and singer best known for her comedic roles in several M-G-M musicals from the 1940s, including *Du Barry Was a Lady*, *The Harvey Girls* with Garland, *Till the Clouds Roll By* with Garland, and *Ziegfeld Follies* with... uhm... Garland.

That great stone face, so pretty, so unmoving...

This was actually her signature trademark, and gained her the nickname "Frozen Face" because early in her career, she once had become practically paralyzed with stage fright before one of her numbers, leading to a hysterical reaction with the audience, who thought it was part of the act.

I first met Virginia at a Western autograph show at a casino in Laughlin, Nevada. She was struggling with a suitcase full of CD's and photos that she was selling at the show. Kasey noticed, and asked me to go over and help her.

I did.

She was very appreciative and in return, wanted to buy me a drink. She did.

Did I mention it was 11 A.M?!!

Virginia was a lot of fun, but she did like to drink!

After the signing, we sat in on a Bingo game and had an absolute ball!

She autographed one of her CD's and gave it to me.

Coincidentally, on the way home from Laughlin, Kasey and I actually came across a genuine "Harvey House" restaurant. We stopped to have a bite to eat. It was fun to say that we'd been, but they look *nothing* like the one in the movie—to be honest, it was more like a down and out *Denny's*.

Virginia lived in a town called Wrightwood nestled among the mountains of Southern California. She had once been its mayor. From time to time she would call me and act as if I were her only friend in the world.

She shared with me how terribly lonesome she had become since the death of her husband in 1996 (she had been married to the first Superman, Kirk Alyn) and that all of her friends were still down in the Los Angeles area.

Suddenly the phone calls stopped and I didn't know what had happened to Virginia.

Later, I found she had passed away on January 16, 2001, and that she had spent her last days at the Motion Picture Home in Woodland Hills. She had been within walking distance of me and I never even knew!

God bless, Virginia, you are missed by me and so many others.

MARGARET O'BRIEN

Another famous M-G-M "O'Brien" I had the pleasure of meeting, was Margaret (no relation to Virginia).

Margaret O'Brien was one of Hollywood's most respected child actors and one of her best roles is that of "Tootie," Judy Garland's youngest sister, in M-G-M's 1944 classic, *Meet Me in St. Louis* for which she won a special Oscar.

Under the Victorian mirror that Margaret O'Brien donated.

One of the most memorable and moving scenes in the entire movie is when the legendary Garland sings "Have Yourself a Merry Little Christmas" to a tear-stained little Margaret.

One Christmas, I was asked to sing in the parlor of the Stagecoach Inn, as I had done at many other Stagecoach events in the past. In my festive repertoire, I planned to include "Have Yourself a Merry Little Christmas." It seemed quite appropriate since the museum was Victorian, and "Meet Me in St. Louis" was set in the Victorian age.

Sometime before this, Margaret O'Brien had donated some beautiful antiques to the Inn and was going to be in attendance that year at the Christmas open house.

I found this out JUST as I was preparing to go on stage.

Now tell me, how do you sing a song to someone that has already had that song sung to them by *THE Judy Garland?* Of course this news made me a nervous wreck, but there was no time to do anything about it. So I took a deep breath and sang it as planned.

To my surprise, it went over quite well, and one of the nicest compliments I've ever received came from Margaret O'Brien that day.

She pulled me aside and said: "Every Christmas, Michael Jackson calls me up and sings that to me. [Pause] *You* do it much better!"

Thank you Margaret! Thank you so very much! That compliment will go with me forever.

I later attended a couple of Christmas Eve parties at the home of Margaret's husband, Roy, in Thousand Oaks, where I was always called on to sing. (Smile).

KATHRYN GRAYSON

"Goddess Extraordinaire"! OK, *second* only to Garland, but Grayson I got to actually meet!

As I mentioned earlier, Kasey and I got tired of beating the proverbial dead horse that *"Bewitched... Again!"* had become, so we COMPLETELY re-wrote the premise into *Son of a Witch!* We both wanted Kathryn Grayson to be one of our witches.

At the time, I was working at a tacky little design shop in the heart of Beverly Hills, and one day when there wasn't much going on at the store, I called the Screen Actors Guild to get a contact number for Kathryn.

I phoned the number and a sweet sounding lady answered the phone. I explained who I was, what the project was about, who was already attached, etc. The lady listened very intently and was most gracious. After I finished, she said she'd pass the information on.

Before I hung up, I finally got around to asking the name of the lady I was speaking with... "Kathryn Grayson"!

I was flabbergasted and didn't know what to say. Miss Grayson just giggled.

Shortly after that, Bernard Fox invited Kathryn for a dinner and show he had set up at the very exclusive, Magic Castle in Hollywood, home to the world's greatest magicians. Kasey delegated me the task of picking up la Grayson.

Alone!

I arrived at her front gate in Westwood and rang the bell. The gate slowly opened. I got out of the car and went to the front door and knocked. The door was opened by her assistant, Sally.

As I entered, I can remember the foyer having very dark wood and lots of red velvet with a grand staircase that swept into view.

It was all *very* Sunset Boulevard!

The lady informed me that Miss Grayson would be right down.

Suddenly there she was... descending the grand staircase just as charming and stunning as can be... sigh!

Once in the car, we had a long travel down Sunset Boulevard to Hollywood. For a short while, we sat in uncomfortable silence. I, for once, was at a loss for words because I was afraid I'd be drooling and babbling on like an idiot.

Finally she turned to me and asked, "Do you know any of my songs?"

"I know ALL of your songs, Miss Grayson."

"Good! Then let's sing!"

If I hadn't been driving I would have DIED on the spot!

So right there, on Sunset Boulevard, I *sang* "Make Believe" and "Be My Love" with the great Kathryn Grayson...(I could still wet my pants over the thought of it...)

We laughed and laughed, and then I told her that when I was doing night club work back in Georgia, my piano player and I would do a bit where he would be "Howard Keel" or "Mario Lanza" and I would be *her*.

Well, THAT began the test... She kept making me sing *higher and higher and higher!!* "Try this note," she'd say. "Now try this one."

Then she began to sing the ending to "Be My Love," and then *I* had to do it.

Finally after a moment of silence, she looked over at me with a big smile and said, "Yep, you can do me!" One note of hers always evaded me. It is at the end of the song "After the Ball" in *Showboat*. I told her it was a note only dogs could hear and she laughed at that!

LIZA!

Tell me, do I *really* need to add the surname?! One weekend, Kasey and I were flown to Florida by our friends Steve and Thomas for an event benefiting AIDS research, and *Liza* was going to be there. At the time, I was in Atlanta visiting my mom for Easter, so I met up with Kasey in Florida.

The night of the party, Liza came walking in. She was on crutches having just had hip surgery and I remember blurting out: "WOW! You look great!" and she replied, "I do???"

We sat at the head table where I was seated next to the rather gruff Mickey Rooney. I actually made the man laugh which is no easy task, let me tell you!

Liza had started to sing "Maybe This Time" and he tearfully leaned over and said to me, "I *loved* her mother." Quietly I whispered back, "Every man in this room loved her mother… In fact, every man in this room wants to be her mother!"

His loud guffaw could be heard all over.

Since then, I've seen him several times, and to this day, he DOES NOT remember me! HA! But still, I always enjoy the fact that I once made Mickey Rooney laugh.

Chapter 30
A Decade with Kasey

Our last trip to the Ranch: July 2005

Kasey used to paraphrase her favorite quote by John Dryden: "I am wounded but not slain and I'll arise to fight again." This was shot in July of 2005 on our last visit to 1164 Morning Glory Circle together. Even with a tracheostomy tube in her neck for air, a G-Tube in her stomach to "eat" and a hundred degrees weather, she was amazingly youthful and active.

2002 saw our 10th anniversary together. I had planned and saved for weeks to be able to buy a diamond and ruby heart shaped necklace for Kasey. I knew she only liked *real* jewelry, so nothing else would do.

That afternoon, we drove up to Oxnard to our favorite Olive Garden restaurant. After dinner was over, she didn't expect the little box that I handed her. After unwrapping it, she saw the rather delicate little necklace.

Then Kasey did something I had NEVER seen her do. She looked at me and began to puddle up! She ran around the table, threw her arms around me, and just kept weeping into my shoulder! But quickly it all turned to laughter when we noticed that everyone was staring! I fastened it around her neck where it stayed until three years later, the night before she was to go in for her huge throat surgery. On the eve of that night, she put the necklace around my neck with explicit instructions it be given back when she was healed. The necklace remains around my neck to this day, more than seven years later as of this writing.

Chapter 31
SPOOKY HAPPENINGS

Kasey and I used to have some unbelievable things happen to us that would pertain to something we were doing or someone we knew, and every time, we'd look at each other and say, "It's a sign! It's a sign!"

For instance, one of those early first days together in '92 we were both in the car going somewhere, and Kasey, a star of *Bewitched*, and me, being the (debatable) number one fan of *Bewitched*, were driving out of a restaurant behind a car whose license plate spelled "BEWITCH." Now I ask you, what are the odds of that?! But these kinds of things happened constantly, and I can't stress enough *how* constantly!

Even though she's now gone, things haven't changed.

In August of 2006, a month after Kasey's passing, I decided to call a psychic who was recommended to me. I had never met this woman: Make of this what you will.

The psychic's name is Cheryl Booth. One of her many gifts is speaking to those who have passed on… (insert creepy music here). Cheryl was living in Phoenix at the time, so she read for me over the phone, recorded our conversation and later sent it to me on CD.

She did not know anything about who I was trying to reach, but quickly determined that it was an "older lady, not a mom, but someone very close" to me.

I asked if *this lady* had been frightened in passing. I was told no; that her brother had been there to meet her. I was a bit stumped. As far as I knew, her brother was alive and well and still living in Burbank.

So I asked his name.

"Charles."

After hearing that, I was a bit blown away. Kasey DID have a half brother named Charles who had passed away many years before. Only her closest family members would even be able to recall his name, and certainly no fan would have known this information.

A moment later Cheryl said that she was seeing a lot of green smoke.

Amazingly she asked, "Is this *Agnes Moorehead*?" I had to laugh and said, "Could be!" Then I asked if she knew who I was trying to reach. She replied "No, but I'm getting initials." Then she said: "Now, she didn't go by these initials, but if I give you a 'K' and a 'C,' you'll know what I'm talking about."

Sheesh!

The reading continued with a few more interesting moments, and then Cheryl said I had a Tiffany lamp in the house. I replied that Kasey and I had several that were that style—table lamps, floor lamps, hanging lamps. "No, this is a table lamp and it sits next to her chair."

This was absolutely true, but how could she possibly know?!

"Kasey is going to try and make that light flicker on and off in the next couple days to let you know she's OK."

Well, now I figured that this gal had really backed herself into a corner. Everything had been pretty interesting up till then, but come on! There's no way that someone who lives in Phoenix, whom I'd never met, could pull this off!

That night I was at my mom's when, adding *injury* to *insult* this time, I fell down her steps and hurt my right foot! But I still drove home.

Remember, our condo was thirty-six steps up from the garage, but I managed to get home that Sunday night and climb all those stairs, only to find out the next day that my right foot was broken!

By Wednesday Mom was staying at the condo helping me out. Later that day, we sat down to watch a movie, Mom sitting in my chair, and me in Kasey's.

Half way through the film, as you might already have guessed, the Tiffany style lamp sitting on the table next to me began to flicker.

My mom and I both stared at it.

The table, the chair and the infamous lamp! *Bewitched* fans may like to know that the shelf above KR's chair was from Elizabeth Montgomery's home. You can see it on the ground in the photo of me at the yard sale on page 147.

Then it began to rapidly *flash* on and off.
Then the bulb blew...
Then it began to smoke...
Then I hobbled over to the breaker!

And by then it was all over. I just know that KR was hysterically laughing at me from "the Ether's"! And what's so great about the whole thing is that I had a witness to all this!! Let's hear it for *Mom*!

Not too far from the condo where Kasey and I lived was a favorite mall of ours that was expanding. Expanding sounds so unimpressive... they *tripled* the size of the place and even installed a two story carousel! Kasey had been looking forward to seeing it when it was all completed. It was to open in the Fall of 2006, but sadly, Kasey wasn't able to wait.

A few days before Christmas that same year, I decided to go see it. As I was walking around, feeling very sad and alone, and thinking of all the wonderful times Kasey and I had together, especially at the holidays, I suddenly *felt* someone take my arm.

Instinctively, I bent my elbow and grasped my shirt front (like gentlemen did in the Victorian days when escorting a lady) as I had done countless times with Kasey through the years.

When I turned and looked, there was no one there and the sensation passed just as fast as it had begun. But for one brief moment, I could *feel* Kasey take my arm one last time, to see the "new" mall with me, and to share one last Christmas moment together. I feel very blessed by that.

Another odd little thing happened in June of 2008, when I was working at my part time gig at Calico Corners.

I was helping out with an inventory, and what do you suppose the odds are that the first two bolts of fabric I started with were named "Lizzie" and "Montgomery"?! HA!

On my 45th birthday, Rose Marie's daughter, "Noopy," found a large yellow and black sign on the side of the road. These types of signs are used to direct people to film shoot locations. They are bright yellow, 16 x 20, have a large black arrow in the middle, and always have one "key" word on the top and bottom. The one Noopy found said "WITCH." She knew she had to get it for me, so late one night she "took" it. We both laughed saying, "It's a sign! It's a sign!" (And it literally was!)

But three days later, as I was exiting the freeway to go to work, there was another one of those identical signs; only this time the one word on it was "TATE"!

Again I ask, what are the odds??? Well, I *had* to have it so I stopped and took it, right in broad daylight!

Now fast-forward a couple of weeks to July 14,th 2008, which was the second anniversary of Kasey's burial. I was feeling really bummed, and for some reason, this particular date bothered me more than June 30th, the date of her stroke, or July 6th, the date of her death.

Kasey must have known that I needed some cheering up, that day, because as I was driving down Ventura Blvd., I happened upon yet another one of those same yellow signs... but this time, there were only *two letters* on it. And of all the combination of letters in the world, this one was "KR."

Yup. It's mine!

One last odd little thing to add to all the others, as it turns out, I recently discovered that David Story, (the young man who first introduced me to Herbie Pilato) and I are fifth cousins on my father's side. That means:

One of my own family members helped introduce me to the cast members of *Bewitched*! But wait...

Odder still, I had never put two and two together before, but my father's mother is a direct relative of the Tobias family of South Carolina, and George Tobias is part of that family, meaning that I am directly related to Abner Kravitz! HA!

Who would have ever believed that members of my own family were part of *Bewitched*?!

Destiny perhaps? One never knows...

FUN SIDE NOTE: Readers may find this strange, but amusing. George Tobias (Abner Kravitz) was actually late for his own funeral! Now this might not have surprised a lot of people who had known him during his last years, because George's mind hadn't quite been what it once was. (Sandy Gould even remembered having to help him remember his lines on "Tabitha"). But as everyone was gathering for George's funeral, George himself never made it! There was literally no *body* because the hearse he was riding in had been *stolen* and was not found for several days! But thankfully there was George, undisturbed and still resting peacefully in the back!

Kasey prepares for battle with an out-of-control bull (ahem...) in Mexico City. She tells it that all the stars of Screen Gems were asked to fight the bull (in reality just a baby that was NOT harmed in anyway). No one would do it so to "save face" she got in the ring. Later on Vito Scotti got into the act also.

Chapter 32
WRAPPING UP THE YEARS

February 2003, Kasey and I attended the first ever TV Land Awards. I have to say it was like pulling teeth to even get the cast of *Bewitched* invited. The fact that Elizabeth Montgomery was gone made them lose interest in the show, but I persevered and they eventually did invite William Asher and Kasey. I, being Kasey's escort, also got to attend.

That night was a lot of fun. I remember one of the categories had something to do with favorite sinister characters and Jeannie's evil twin sister won out over Serena... (perhaps because Barbara was on hand) Through the magic of special effects, both "Jeannies" *were there* to accept the award! This is all from the same network that ran the same contest year after year... to find out who was more powerful; Samantha or Jeannie. For those of you who don't know who won that contest each and every time, look it up. *Tinka-tinka-tee*!

I also remember that one of the things TV Land edited out of the final broadcast was David Cassidy asking the audience if they noticed that "the only people winning awards were those still alive?" (I guess that didn't sit too well with the Powers That Be!)

That same night was not without its embarrassing moments courtesy of yours truly.

Right before the show started, I went to the men's room. There were three urinals on the wall and the two outer ones were in use. Shyly, I took my place in the middle. Only then did I realize who I was standing between. After a moment of awkward silence I asked, "Do you guys know how hard it is to pee between Mr. Spock and The 6 Million Dollar Man?!" Leonard Nimoy and Lee Majors both started to laugh and Nimoy said: "Tell me if he (Majors) does it in slow motion!"

A stunning KR at the first annual TV Land Awards

Me and Shirley (Partridge) Jones.

Later, the subject of Jack Cassidy came up that night between Kasey and me. During the conversation it dawned on me that if you take the "I,D,Y" off of "Jack Cassidy", you end up with "*JACK-ASS*"! And yes, I said it out loud.

Immediately I heard a loud guffaw behind me and it was then that I realized Shirley Jones and Marty Ingels were standing within earshot. I was a little embarrassed and most apologetic, but they thought it was funny, especially Marty. 2003 also saw a star for William Asher (November 22). Not in Hollywood, which is one of the crimes of the century—make that TWO centuries now—but in Palm Springs' version of the Walk of Fame. SueAne had gotten one there on her birthday, March 8, 1997.

Kasey and I were invited to attend and we stood alongside the adorable Henry Gibson from *Laugh-In*. Henry once had played Napoleon on an episode of *Bewitched*. Paul Lynde has the greatest line in that: "Stand up... (He is)... all the way!"

Bill Asher, KR and me at Bill's star dedication.

The after-party was a lot of fun and it was here that I really got to meet the rest of the Asher family. I still treasure my little star-shaped pin with Bill's name that I received that day.

SueAne Langdon received a star there as well, on her birthday, March 8, 1997. So if you're ever out "star-gazing" in Palm Springs, look for Bill and SueAne's, which were both well-deserved and long overdue and just across the side street from each other.

August of 2004 it was my turn to go in for surgery. Lasik eye surgery, that is. Kasey was right outside the operating room as I lay in a complete panic on a table in a room that was freezing! I thought I wouldn't live just out of fear alone… but I have to honestly say that if you're considering the surgery, go for it, because much to my surprise, it didn't hurt a bit!

Kasey had waited until I had "healed" before she told me that she was concerned about her throat, which at the time we both thought was strictly a fibrosis issue brought on by a lot of radiation therapies.

Kasey and Henry!

In the early days, most doctors didn't believe or understand that radiation caused this problem, so they did NOT bother putting patients on any kind of regimen to keep it from becoming debilitating. Sadly, Kasey was one of those, as she was slowly being robbed of the ability to swallow.

She asked me to feel her neck and throat area.

When I did, I was stunned.

The entire area felt like a solid concrete brick covered with a thin layer of tissue paper!

I also couldn't understand why she had waited so long to say anything. I later found out that both fear and denial were running rampant through her mind.

Despite all that was going on, we still held our annual Halloween party at the Stagecoach Inn Museum that year, and on November 1st Kasey and I shot a pilot for a proposed series based on our craft books called "Hands-on Holidays."

That September, we also shot a spooky, Victorian-style commercial for the yearly Halloween party that benefited the museum.

Rose Marie and Bernard at the Stagecoach Inn in 2005

Chapter 32: Wrapping Up The Years

Greeting you at the front door was SueAne Langdon, dressed in a gorgeous, brown, silk bustle-gown.

Rose Marie conducted the séance; complete with flickering lights, banging doors, and a *live* ghost! Seven lucky visitors got to sit at the dining room table with her and partake.

Margaret O'Brien was in the upstairs bedroom with a haunted cradle that began to rock after she put down "her" invisible baby.

I sang the old Bing Crosby Disney song, "The Headless Horseman" in the parlor, and at one point I forgot the lyrics! I looked over and for some reason, it just dawned on me that there stood SueAne Langdon, playing my "wife." After all those years of knowing her, it still blew my mind that I was doing a scene with SueAne Langdon! The party was a great success.

By that Christmas, we knew that Kasey had more than just a fibrosis problem. Her throat cancer had returned.

One of the hardest things you'll ever do in life is go with your partner, spouse, or best friend, to a cemetery and pick out plots, caskets, grave markers and flowers. But that's what Kasey and I did.

Not knowing if she would even survive the upcoming surgery, she insisted on making sure that everything was taken care of.

Kasey was operated on by Dr. Sinha, an incredible physician at USC, who would be performing an incredibly complicated procedure.

He had to remove tissue from Kasey's left wrist as well as part of the main artery. Afterwards, he *removed* her *entire throat* along with all the surrounding cancerous tissue. He then *replaced* her throat with the tissue he took from her wrist. Many long hours later, we finally got the word that Kasey had come through beautifully.

The following year and a half that followed now seems like a blur.

As I touched on before, Kasey had a tracheostomy tube that needed constant cleaning. We employed everything from tweezers to Q-Tips, as well as a suction machine that was constantly in use.

She was fed through a G-Tube to her stomach for the rest of her life which entailed the same cleaning and wound dressing.

But I'll tell you, she was innovative! We would get Marie Callender's Chicken pot pies, add milk, and then put it in this blender we found that could've ground up a tree branch!

Taking care of the trach and the G-Tube feedings became a very personal thing to Kasey. She didn't want anyone else to do it except me—not even members of her own family.

She also had a little bell to ring for me during the night, which we later supplemented with a Walkie-Talkie that had a button that would do the same thing.

There were countless times I would have to go to her room in the middle of the night because her dinner had come back up. She would clean herself up and I would take care of all the bedding and put her back to bed.

Many nights I would lay there with her until she fell back asleep. We were close before, but we became even more so at this point.

Only twice did I ever see her really fall apart, because that just wasn't her style. Kasey was always very accepting and knew how to proceed with her life.

We were given tons of exercises to do to try and help her be able to swallow again. The "K" sound, for instance, is formed when the throat comes together at the point where it swallows. So one of her exercises was to repeat words after me that ended in a "K" sound: truck, black, pick, Mark, Mike, Quack, (that was one of her favorites) and we'd always end that exercise with "DICK YORK"! We always tried to make it fun and sometimes would find ourselves laughing through the whole thing! Especially when she would holler F*CK!

Our last Halloween together was actually a fun time as well. I bought tickets to see a King Tut exhibit at the Los Angeles County Museum. The day was dreary and the weather kept threatening rain, but the air was still comfortable for late October. After we had gone through the exhibit, we walked over to the Marie Callender's Restaurant right next to the La Brea Tar Pits on Wilshire Blvd. We sat together on the same side of the booth, as we had for so long, so I could feed Kasey through the G-Tube without a lot of people noticing.

We decided to order our favorite Cosmopolitan drinks. This was the first time I had ever put one straight into her G-Tube, and the effect was darn near immediate!

We ate... or rather, *I* ate, and we laughed at everything and probably had the best time we had had, since all the cancer crap had begun! It truly is still one of my favorite memories.

Such a long distance from the first Halloween we spent together.

That December was one of the hardest and busiest months I've ever spent. Kasey would be turning 80 and she wanted a party... a party to say "thank you, and I love you" to all her family and friends.

By this point, I was totally exhausted and told her kids that I just couldn't handle it by myself. But as it turned out, I pretty much

ended up having to do it all anyway. SueAne offered her lovely backyard, so we got heat lamps and rented tables and chairs.

The decorations would be pink and white linens, a pink poinsettia placed in the center of every table, and hundreds of glittery clear snowflakes in several sizes.

At the last moment, a bit of inspiration came over me and I got 80 silver frames in various sizes and made copies of 80 different pictures of Kasey from her birth to now. The photos, along with tea lights, were placed everywhere.

The food was served inside, buffet style, and sat on a table that was also loaded with pink poinsettias and black and white pictures in silver frames.

It was lovely.

Several of the Ashers came, as well as the Fox's. This was also the last Christmas we would get to spend with Bernard and Jacque's daughter, Valerie. I got in touch with a couple of *Bewitched* fans (who have since become close friends): Mark Simpson, his friend Ross, and Ross' friend Paul, to come down from Seattle and help out with the bartending and picture taking.

Poor Mark Simpson, being such a huge *Bewitched* fan, he seemed incredibly flustered when I asked him to pick Kasey up for the party that night and bring her to SueAne's. When he arrived at our condo, he found her standing outside in her fur coat waiting on the curb! This was his first introduction to Louise Tate!

I spent days prior at SueAne's decorating for the party, at the same time decorating our own condo for Christmas, all the while trying to keep up with Kasey's schedule, as well as working at Rose Marie's!

And then there was Wink.

Our little dog had been sick, and had been trying to tell me for days that it was time for him to leave. I just couldn't bear the thought. I used to take him over to SueAne's every day while I was decorating, and put him on a towel in the sun. I even made his favorite meal—pan browned chicken, and would try and feed it to him. But nothing was working. Wink was slipping away.

I finally made myself face up to it, so I took Wink to the vet.

I was told what I had been afraid to hear. The time had come to say goodbye to my little boy. Kasey's daughter Monika had been driving her to a doctor's appointment and turned around to come back and be with me.

It was all so unbearable.

It was also Kasey's birthday, December 15th. Luckily her party was not until the following Sunday.

I had to let Wink go in the midst of all this other trouble and heartache.

I will forever be grateful to Monika. She paid to have Wink cremated, and I still have him with me. Someday I will scatter his few ashes over the lake here in Calabasas where he so loved to walk.

One night, not too long after the party, but still before Christmas, Kasey and I came home to find a gift on the front porch. Sitting behind that gift was a black cat with white feet.

Me and Wink

That cat, who was wearing a name tag that said "Toonsy," instantly came up to me and would not leave my side. It was strange.

After Kasey went in, I sat there on the porch for more than an hour with that cat on my lap. He seemed to want to comfort me as I cried. Inside, the condo never looked lovelier, but it wasn't a very Merry Christmas.

I tried to take the cat home to its owner, a lady named Judy Unell, who lived behind us in the Motion Picture Home. She was 90 years old at the time but you'd never know it!

But that cat would not leave. He wouldn't come in the house, yet he wouldn't leave. Both my neighbor Anna, whose 46 year old fiancé was fighting adult leukemia, and I began feeding Toonsy. He became like therapy to us. Anna was going through the cancer treatments with her fiancé, while I was going through the treatments with Kasey. We'd even run into each other from time to time at the hospitals.

On one particularly cold night, I peeked out the door and found Toonsy sitting there. I opened the door and told him to "come in."

He finally did and he never left. He slept right next to me from then on.

That was the Christmas I gave Kasey the matching earrings to the heart shaped diamond and ruby necklace I had given her on our tenth anniversary. I placed them in a silver painted walnut shell and hung them on the tree.

Chapter 33
Poignant Goodbyes

By Christmas and her birthday, Kasey and I knew that, after all of our efforts, her cancer had returned, and we weren't telling anyone because of the Christmas season.

There's no delicate way of saying these things so why try?

By March, our neighbor, Anna's fiancé, died.

In May, we lost Valerie Fox.

On June 30th, Kasey suffered a stroke and died on July 6th.

Not a moment goes by without a thought of her. I miss her so.

It had only been six months since I had also lost Wink, and within the year I would also lose Toonsy, that incredible cat that had come to my emotional rescue just a year before.

Damn coyotes.

Those were some of the lowest moments of my life. It seemed that everyone and everything that I loved was gone. My best friend and soul mate, my home, my reasons for even being in Los Angeles and soon the home Kasey and I shared and did so much in would be sold.

It's not always easy trying to go on with your life when you've lost those you love, especially that seemingly once in a lifetime soul mate; but we must.

I'm thankful for every minute Kasey and I shared together and I wouldn't trade it for the world. I'm also thankful for good friends and a sense of humor, which helps me get through the lonely times and face each day with a smile, and in doing so, I honor Kasey's memory, because that's exactly what she would have wanted me to do.

Last photo together.

Epilogue

As of this writing, it's been six years since Kasey's passing. I continue to work with Rose Marie, taking her to doctor appointments, grocery stores and functions. I fuss at her when she insists on eating things that are not good for her, but I know she respects me for standing up to her and telling her so. I can honestly say that I make her laugh... a lot.

L-R Sid Caesar, Dick Van Dyke, Rose Marie, and Me at the 80th birthday party of director John Rich.

One day while we were out driving, it began to get very cloudy outside, yet it was still quite hot. She commented on the clouds, which immediately reminded me of a famous movie quote, so I turned to her and in my most tragic Bette Davis voice said, "*Yet I can still feel the sun on the back of my hands...*"

We both burst into hysterics. Rose Marie was taken aback that I knew this classic line from the Bette Davis movie, *Dark Victory*.

We still throw that line around constantly, and laugh like school kids!

Kasey's grave marker was finally put in place in June 2008. Bewitched fans the world over will be pleased to know that engraved on it is Kasey's favorite quote from Bewitched in raised, bronze letters:

"WE ARE QUICK SILVER, A FLEETING SHADOW, A DISTANT SOUND.
OUR HOME HAS NO BOUNDARIES BEYOND WHICH WE CANNOT PASS.
WE LIVE IN MUSIC—A FLASH OF COLOR.
WE LIVE ON THE WIND AND IN THE SPARKLE OF A STAR."

For as long as I've known her, she always wanted that quotation on her gravestone for the entire world to see.

She felt it transcended *Bewitched* and applied to anyone who has ever truly *lived*. Kasey Rogers was one of those rare individuals that did just that—she *truly* lived.

As for me, my dreams most certainly *did* come true.

Kasey once told me, "Mark, you may not have gotten a TV series out of this, but when you can make the professionals like Bernard Fox and Rose Marie laugh, *you* are a success!"

Meeting Kasey literally changed my life... Sometimes I find it hard to believe myself that I lived with Louise Tate, ate dinner with Gladys Kravitz, attended the funeral of Darrin AND Samantha Stephens, and became like a son to Dr. Bombay. I also have the incredible honor of calling dozens of stars from my childhood *friends*.

I am a success because of Kasey. She will always be the sparkle of my star.

There are literally thousands of photos in my collection that I would love to share but I'm told that is impossible! HA! So the following are just a few that I thought you may like to see. I didn't really have full stories to go with them so I'll just put them here with a caption.

Sandra Gould peruses her book *Always Say Maybe*.

With *Bewitched*'s art director Ross Bellah. Ross was also responsible for Jeannie's bottle and still had a cupful of the large jewels used for the interior of Jeannie's bottle on his kitchen windowsill!

Here I am shooting my first ever commercial in Los Angeles, oddly enough on the same soundstage that once housed *Bewitched*!

Endora makes a "guest appearance" after Sandy and Kasey fool around with the Ouija Board on Halloween! I made that outfit for my friend Scott and the next year turned him into Witchiepoo!

With Rose Marie celebrating singer Kay Starr's 85th birthday

At an '05 premier party for a film called *Bullets Over Broadway* with Rose Marie and Margaret O'Brien.

Kasey meets up with Spidey on my 33rd birthday!

Lost in a Halloween Corn Maze with Rose Marie!

Epilogue

Kasey was never above anything! Here she is sanding our new wood floor that we were self-installing in the condo! To my knowledge, what we wrote under it still lies there!

Kasey and I reenact her famous scene on the actual lake from *Strangers on A Train*... I get to be the psychotic Robert Walker! Ha!

Rose Marie with a few of her many treasures she still had from her career. In January of 2008 I got her inducted into the Smithsonian Institute. She donated the small ruffled dress and gold shoes that she wore in 1927 in her very first all singing Vitaphone short! Also, a bow from the *Dick Van Dyke Show* days.

Acknowledgments

Thanks goes to my Mom. More than 20 years ago she and my Dad put me on a plane to come out here. She tear'd up and hugged me tight. I believe she knew before I did that I would not return home from that journey. I would also like to thank ALL those, both still here and not, mentioned in the body of this text or not, that shaped those wonderful 15 years: Sandy Gould, Bernard, Jacque, Amanda, Valerie Fox, Lisa Wilkie, Dick Sargent, Rose Marie, SueAne Langdon, Annette Boyer, Scott Awley, Steven Colbert, Keith Jennings, Gilmore Rizzo, Julia DelJudge, Noopy and Steve, Kathy Vigoda, Maret Wicken, Gloria Solari and the many different casts of Calico Corners. I'd also like to thank Ben Ohmart, publisher of BearManor Media, Sandra Grabman, production manager and Valerie Thompson for the design of this book.

This list could go on and on… if I missed you, my apologies and thank you.

And one last note of thanks. To Kasey Rogers, where ever you are I hope you can see this. I loved you. I miss you.

How I like to remember them. Shot on October 5th, 1967.

INDEX

Always Say Maybe – 89, 189
Asher, Meredith – 149
Asher, William – 7, 9, 43, 149, 150, 173, 175, 176
Bellah, Ross – 190
Bewitched – 2, 3, 11-13, 16, 26, 33, 41, 43, 44, 46, 49-51, 61, 63, 74-76, 86, 89, 90, 94, 97-99, 102, 104, 105, 113, 115, 119, 121-124, 128, 133-138, 144, 149-151, 153, 167, 169, 171, 173, 175, 183, 188, 190
Bewitched... Again – 1, 2, 10, 12, 57, 61, 72, 128, 135, 138, 153, 161
Bewitched Cookbook – 1, 113, 114, 121, 128
Calabasas, CA – 183
Cancer – 3, 45, 99, 100, 125, 126, 136, 180, 181, 184, 185
Ceaser, Sid – 187
Clift, Montgomery – 25, 26
Columbia Pictures – 15, 16, 121
DeCarlo, Yvonne – 32, 33
Denver and the Rio Grande – 30, 34, 35
Designing Women – 127, 128

Earthquake – 81, 94
Eden, Barbara – 99
Endora – 48, 49, 122, 124, 191
Forest Lawn – 137
Fox, Bernard – 3, 7, 21, 33, 74, 86, 90, 93, 101-109, 115, 119, 137, 144, 146, 162, 178, 183, 188, 199
Freeman, Kathleen – 75
Ghostley, Alice – 46, 107, 127-130, 137
Gibson, Henry – 175, 177
Golden Circle – 25, 26
Gould, Sandra – 21, 45-48, 61, 74, 77, 85-99, 104, 126, 135, 137, 139, 150, 171, 189, 191, 199
Granger, Farley – 28
Grayson, Kathryn – 161-163
Hedren, Tippi – 30-31
Hitchcock, Alfred – 226, 29, 30, 56
Hitchcock, Pat – 30, 31
Hollywood – 1, 15, 21, 25, 28, 30, 40, 57, 61, 82, 83, 89, 90, 119, 121, 126, 129, 135, 137, 157, 159, 162, 163, 175
Hollywood Forever Memorial Park – 63

I Dream of Jeannie – 16, 99, 100, 173, 190
Ingels, Marty – 175
Jones, Shirley – 175
Kravitz, Abner – 12, 46, 86, 97, 105, 171
Kravitz, Gladys – 12, 21, 45, 46, 85-87, 150, 188
Langdon, SueAne – 7, 8, 83, 84, 99, 100, 175, 176, 179, 180, 182, 183, 199
Laura Elliott – 23, 25, 26, 28, 29, 30-34, 36
Leigh, Janet – 32
Lorne, Marion – 16
MGM Studios – 121, 122, 157, 159
Minnelli, Liza – 163, 164
Montgomery, Elizabeth – 9, 12, 26, 43, 46-48, 61, 99, 113, 134, 137, 138, 144, 146, 147, 149-151, 169, 173
Moorehead, Agnes – 119, 121-124, 168
Morse, Hollingsworth – 93, 94
Murphy, Erin – 61, 101, 135, 137
Edmund O'Brien – 32, 34
O'Brien, Margaret – 159-161, 179, 192
O'Brien, Virginia – 157
Paramount Studios – 18, 19, 22-26, 29, 30, 36, 89, 115
Pearce, Alice – 45, 46, 150
Peyton Place – 39, 41, 42, 44, 51
Rich, John – 187
Ringling Bros Barnum & Bailey Circus – 85, 86
Rogers, Kasey – 1-3, 7, 10, 12, 13, 15-19, 21, 23—25, 28-30, 32, 33, 35, 36, 39-44, 46—51, 53-57, 60-65, 67-69, 71-73, 75-77, 79-86, 89, 94, 96, 97-105, 108, 109, 111, 113-116, 119, 121, 122, 124, 125-128, 131, 135, 137-139, 141, 142, 144, 149-151, 153, 154, 158, 159, 161-163, 165-168, 170, 171, 173, 175-178, 180-185, 187, 188, 191, 193, 195, 196, 199
Roman, Ruth – 30
Rose Marie – 1, 74, 116, 170, 178, 179, 183, 187, 188, 192, 194, 198, 199
Salem, MA – 12, 74, 134, 135
Samantha Statue – 134
Sargent, Dick – 44, 61, 134, 139, 153, 199
Screen Gems – 50
Sex, Pots and Pans – 89
Silver City – 32, 33
Smithsonian – 198
Smyrna, GA – 10, 15, 16
Son of a Witch – 1, 71, 72, 74, 161
Springer, Jerry – 99, 101, 102
Stagecoach Inn Museum – 84, 414, 412, 160, 178
Starr, Kay – 192
Stephens, Darrin – 9, 10, 12, 16, 44, 41, 48, 49, 52, 121, 133, 134, 136-138, 140, 153, 157, 188
Stephens, Samantha – 3, 9, 10, 12, 46, 48, 49, 52, 74, 94, 99, 109, 113, 134, 137, 150, 151, 173, 188
Stranger's on a Train – 26, 28-31, 196
Sunset Boulevard – 21, 83, 89, 163

Sunset/Gower – 15
Tabatha – 10, 101
Tabitha – 94, 171
Tate, Larry – 43, 44, 48, 51, 54
Tate, Louise – 7, 10, 12, 13, 30, 43-45, 48, 49-51, 54, 76, 97, 101, 128, 149, 151, 183, 188
Taylor, Elizabeth – 25, 26, 29
Tobias, George – 46, 171
Two Lost Worlds – 36, 41

Van Dyke, Dick – 1, 116, 187, 198
Vernon, Irene – 43, 149
Walker, Robert – 28, 29, 31, 196
Webb, Clifton – 63
Westport, CT – 39, 43, 134
White, David – 48, 63, 149
Wink – 59, 60, 79, 81, 183, 184, 185
Women's Motocross – 53-56
York, Dick – 9, 181

www.ingramcontent.com/pod-product-compliance
Lightning Source LLC
Chambersburg PA
CBHW050758160426
43192CB00010B/1559